MARCO ⊕ POLO

T0148727

PA RIS

GREAT BRITAIN — BELGIUM

LUX.

Paris

GER.

Seine

Loire

Dijon

Rhine

Nantes

SWITZ.

FRANCE

Lyon

ITALY

Rhône

Bordeaux

Marseilles

SPAIN — AND.

Mediter ranean

www.marco-polo.com

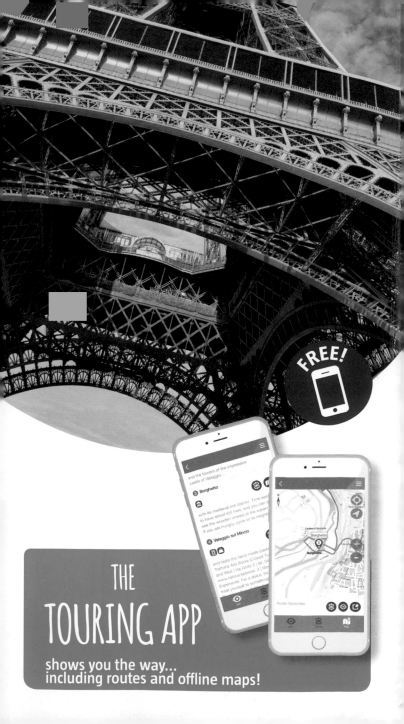

GET MORE OUT OF YOUR MARCO POLO GUIDE

IT'S AS SIMPLE AS THIS

1 go.marco-polo.com/par

2 download and discover

GO!

WORKS OFFLINE!

SYMBOLS

INSIDER TIP Insider Tip

★ Highlight

●●●● Best of...

ᶰᶩᶤ Scenic view

♲ Responsible travel: for ecological or fair trade aspects

(*) Telephone numbers that are not toll-free

PRICE CATEGORIES HOTELS

Expensive	over 160 euros
Moderate	100–160 euros
Budget	under 100 euros

Prices are for two people in a double room per night without breakfast

PRICE CATEGORIES RESTAURANTS

Expensive	over 60 euros
Moderate	35–60 euros
Budget	under 35 euros

Prices are for an evening menu with starter, main course and dessert, without wine

On the cover: Shopping arcade in the art temple p. 38 | Picnic along the Canal Saint-Martin p. 25

CONTENTS

MAPS IN THE GUIDEBOOK
(136 A1) Page numbers and coordinates refer to the street atlas, the map of the districts and the map of Greater Paris

(0) Site/address located off the map
Coordinates are also given for places that are not marked on the street atlas

(ℳ A1) refers to the removable pull-out map

INSIDE FRONT COVER:
The best Highlights

INSIDE BACK COVER:
Metro/RER map

The best MARCO POLO Insider Tips

Our top 15 Insider Tips

INSIDER TIP Monets, Monets, Monets

The *Musée Marmottan* houses more than 100 works by Claude Monet, including the famous painting that gave Impressionism its name. The museum also displays part of the private art collection of this master artist. It is located in a park only a stone's throw from the Eiffel Tower → **p. 56**

INSIDER TIP Refreshingly fizzy

Not only do most restaurants serve tap water for free – you can also find *drinking fountains* throughout the entire city. Seven of them even produce carbonated water at the touch of a button! → **p. 22**

INSIDER TIP Game of chance

At the *Le Hasard Ludique* cultural centre, chance is the name of the game, so to speak. Perhaps, by chance, one of the hot concerts or DJ sets there will interest you → **p. 87**

INSIDER TIP Antiques stroll

Rummage through odds and ends from granny's attic in the assortment of back-to-back antique shops, handicraft shops and cafés in the *Village Saint-Paul* area → **p. 74**

INSIDER TIP Next stop: jazz

Live concerts in an old train station concourse. People don't come to *La Gare* to chat; the focus is on the music → **p. 89**

INSIDER TIP Twilight tour with dinner

What could be more romantic than an evening cruise on the Seine? Dinner on the *Calife* is a real treat → **p. 66**

INSIDER TIP The book bar

As the name *Le Barbouquin* indicates, in addition to drinks, this bar offers books, books and more books. Here in Belleville – home to street artists – is where the 21st-century Parisian literati meet → **p. 63**

BEST OF...

FOR FREE

● *Atmospheric organ concerts*
A number of churches regularly offer free concerts. The rich sound of organ music resonating through the arches of *Notre-Dame Cathedral* is more than impressive – both visually and acoustically → p. 33

● *Free couscous*
The *Le Tribal-Café* as well as a dozen or so other restaurants provide a free meal. However, guests are expected to pay a small amount for a beverage → p. 85

● *It's good to be young*
Cultural events and institutions are often free for young people. Why spend money on theatre tickets when they can attend performances like the ones at the *Comédie Française* for free on certain days? → p. 91

● *Free museum admission*
Many museums in Paris do not charge admission. One of the most highly recommended is the *Musée d'Art Moderne de la Ville de Paris* → p. 31

● *Free Paris view*
For the best view of the city without paying admission tor the Eiffel Tower or the Tour Montparnasse climb the stairs of *Sacré-Cœur* (photo) → p. 57

● *Paris on inline skates*
Every Friday evening, nearly 20 miles of the city are closed off for Rollerbladers. Inline skating is an enjoyable way of getting to know Paris. The fun begins at 10pm at Montparnasse station → p. 88

● *Live chansons for joining in*
Several modest restaurants – e.g. *Le Vieux Belleville* – provide diners with affordable meals and live concerts. You can join in when they hand out lyric sheets → p. 71

◖◖◖◗ Dots in guidebook refer to "Best of..." tips

● *Gourmet mecca*

Nowhere else in the world have so many stars graced both chefs and restaurants as in Paris. Yet the *brasseries* such as *Bofinger* are still the gastronomic heart of the city, offering the best quality plus an amazing ambiance → p. 61

● *Arcades – Nostalgie à la française*

Paris is defined by the splendour of its past. Upscale covered shopping centres such as the *Galerie Vivienne* (photo) have existed since the 18th century and are typical of parts of the city even today → p. 42

● *Inner city market with multicultural flair*

Chinese, Indians and Africans from every part of the continent have all injected culture and an exotic flair into certain districts. The African market, *Marché Barbès*, is a tantalising example → p. 81

● *Luxurious shopping*

Paris, as the epitome of luxury, is celebrated for its champagne, perfume and fashion. You can find a large selection of luxury items within the "Triangle d'Or" – the golden triangle around the *rue du Faubourg Saint-Honoré* → p. 79

● *Museums of international renown*

Alongside the Louvre – the museum with the largest exhibition space in the world – the Centre Pompidou boasts the largest collection of modern art in Europe today. The museum that best reflects Paris, however, is the *Musée d'Orsay*, with its collection of works by the French Impressionists → p. 39

● *Street cafés*

Street cafés act as an extension of a Parisian living room. Even the tiniest space on the pavement has enough room for a couple of tables and chairs. The café terrace at the *Café Marly* at the Louvre is ideal for people-watching → p. 65

● *Film set*

Even if you've never been to Paris, you've probably seen the city on the big screen. Around 900 film shoots are held in Paris every year; you can visit the locations where many popular films were shot → p. 20

ONLY IN

BEST OF...

● **Covered shopping centres**
There are numerous department stores and covered passages that are ideal for souvenir hunting during a downpour. The *Carrousel du Louvre* is architecturally stunning and its shops are open on Sundays → p. 36

● **Jungle in the city**
The *greenhouses* in the Jardin des Plantes are a tribute to the resplendent Belle Époque. The lush vegetation will revive your spirits on a damp rainy day in Paris → p. 119

● **Browse and listen in this bookstore**
You'll need plenty of time to shop for CDs, books and DVDs at the most ideal venue, *Fnac*. It is located on the Champs-Elysées and stays open until midnight → p. 74

● **Museum of foreign cultures**
Have you already ticked off all the "must-sees" from your list of museums? If these didn't include the impressive *Musée Quai Branly – Jacques Chirac,* it's worth spending an entire day in this foreign cultural environment – and you still won't have seen everything → p. 32

● **Be part of the aristocracy in this restaurant**
While away the time until the sun reappears in the midst of gilded pageantry at the most beautiful railway station restaurant in the world, *Le Train Bleu* (photo). You don't even need to have a meal there to experience its grandeur – let yourself be enraptured by the sumptuousness of the comfortable leather chairs → p. 65

● **Go underground**
The "underworld" in Paris is extensive, not only for the Métro and sewage system, but also the *catacombs*, an over 300 km (186 mile)-long system of tunnels for the dead → p. 54

RAIN

RELAX AND CHILL OUT
Take it easy and spoil yourself

● *Green urban oases*
Paris is known for its parks that are oases of calm in the boisterous city. The most beloved of them is the *Jardin du Luxembourg* (photo), where you can always find a quiet spot to dream → **p. 50**

● *Luxury hotel spa package*
Some luxury hotels offer an all-inclusive pampering package. The *L'Hôtel* is a real gem, complete with hamam and a pool under the arches, reminiscent of an ancient Roman spa → **p. 93**

● *Tranquil beauty in the church courtyard*
Seek contemplation and relaxation among the tombs of famous poets, painters and musicians, surrounded by nature. Paris' cemeteries, especially the lovely *Père Lachaise* with its majestic trees, are the epitome of serenity → **p. 55**

● *Teatime*
Tea is in popular demand. The *Maison de Thé George Cannon* in particular is devoted to this calming and stimulating herb. Once you've tasted the tea on the ground floor, treat yourself to a shiatsu massage. In the basement you'll find not only a tea shop, but also an original Japanese tea ceremony → **p. 76**

● *Relax on the beach*
Every summer the Seine promenades are piled up with sand. When the *Paris plages* open, they are closed to traffic to create a relaxing beach atmosphere in the heart of the city → **p. 120**

● *Picnics along the canal*
A row of bars line the *Canal Saint-Martin* like a strand of pearls, while the opposite bank of the canal has been converted into a huge picnic area. Sitting on the waterfront on a mild summer night offers a particular Parisian flair → **p. 25**

INTRODUCTION

DISCOVER PARIS!

Paris has been called the city of love, fashion, gastronomy, art and even the city of lights. It has always been a metropolis where only the best is good enough, a city of superlatives. Faster, prettier, bigger, glossier than most other cities. All it takes is a stroll along the magnificent mile-long Champs-Elysées illuminated by *hundreds of thousands of lights* on a December evening or a coffee at a street café as you watch the colourful hustle and bustle of the vibrant Saint-Germain-des-Prés district at all hours with its exuberant student life and many nightclubs to be infected by the charm of this city.

Paris consists of 20 districts, known as arrondissements, that expand out in a spiral from the 1st arrondissement at the heart of the city. Parisians associate very specific clichés with each arrondissement number. The 16th arrondissement, for example, is synonymous with the bourgeoisie, while the 11th is coolness personified. Conveniently, street signs always also indicate which arrondissement you're currently located in. You'll start to spot the clichés that characterise the individual arrondissements yourself pretty quickly. At 105.4 km² (40.7 square miles), Paris is far less than a tenth of the geographical size of Greater London, making it a highly walkable or bikeable city.

Bateaux mouches, tourist boats, on the Seine, Musée d'Orsay to starboard and Pont Royal ahead

The Seine divides the city into *rive gauche* in the south and *rive droite* in the north. There's also a societal dividing line between the well-to-do districts in the west and the poorer quarters in the east of the city.

You can get a good overview of the city from the observation platform on the sixth floor of the *Centre Georges Pompidou,* which lies in the middle of the city centre and high enough up that you can take in the sea of buildings. The city spreads out like an open history book beneath you. The bright mobile sculptures and cascading water of the Stravinsky Fountain lie at your feet and, further up, the towers of the famous Notre-Dame Cathedral loom into view. It stands on the Île de la Cité, the actual nucleus of the city where the Parisii settled in the 3rd century BC. A bit further afield you'll recognise the defiant towers of the former prison, la Conciergerie. Even further beyond and slightly to the right, you can see the sprawling giant complex of the Louvre, a former royal palace that now houses the *largest museum in the world*.

> **Paris has been the stage for many revolutions**

To the right behind you is the sparkling golden dome of Les Invalides in which Napoleon found his final resting place. Not far away the symbol of the city, the Eiffel Tower, looms on the horizon. To the far right and to the west you can pick out the high-rises in La Défense, *Europe's largest office district*. Look further to the right and north to where the dazzling white church, Sacré-Cœur, crowns the highest peak of the former artists' hill, Montmartre.

Paris has been the vibrant political, economical and cultural epicentre of France for centuries and one of the largest metropolises in the world. As the residence of kings and the seat of government and by virtue of its numerous universities, Paris was also recognised as an *intellectual centre in Europe* as far back as the Middle Ages. It has been the workplace for countless artists, writers and architects and a continual source of unrest and uprisings. Paris was the stage for many revolutions. The great revolution of 1789, known for its motto "liberty, equality, fraternity", even became a symbol for the fight against oppression, although the rights championed mostly benefited the bourgeoisie and not the lower classes. Nevertheless, the French Revolution became a guiding light for freedom movements in many countries. Strikes and demonstrations still frequently occur in Paris and, even if they no longer have universal historical significance, every French government still fears mobilisation in the streets.

What gives Paris its special flair? For some, it's the *grand boulevards* so ideal for strolling. For others it's the lure of luxury boutiques on the rue du Faubourg Saint-Honoré or shopping in *world-renowned department stores* such as Galeries Lafayette or Printemps, famed for their extravagant Christmas decorations. Others are content to explore the incredible variety of *museums of international renown*, stroll along the Seine, sit in a street café or relax in one of the many parks – or just go with the flow. Even the older, the provincial, almost rural and unvarnished Paris still exists: attractive alleyways, crooked little buildings with cafés or pleasant restaurants, shops with enticing displays and chattering shopkeepers, the hubbub of activity wherever fresh produce is delivered, and *fascinating markets* with their typically colourful displays of fruit and vegetables, cheese, sausages and meat, pastries and cakes whose vendors loudly tout their wares. This folksy side of Paris is typical north and east of the city, for example in Belleville, which is inhabited by a large number of immigrants, but also artists and young families, since living costs are still affordable here. Experience art for free in an outdoor setting: Rue Denoyez is *the* spot for *graffiti and street artists*, who bring some colour to the

Famous department stores and museums of international renown

grey of this working-class neighbourhood. Hidden behind modern residential blocks, winding alleys like Villa de l'Ermitage and Cité Leroy – with their tiny houses – give us a glimpse of how the area must have looked in the 19th century. The hilltop neighbourhood of Butte aux Cailles has also maintained some of its old-world charm; its bistros and affordable restaurants attract a younger Parisian crowd.

Paris has always had a colourful mixture of people from various backgrounds. Centuries ago, it was the Bretons, Auvergneses, Alsatians and Basques who came to Paris in search of a better life that enriched the city – it was the Alsatians who first introduced their brasseries. Much later, Africans arrived who maintain a wonderfully colourful market in Goutte d'Or every Sunday, and the Chinese, who settled in Place d'Italie where they opened their markets, businesses and restaurants. Paris is multicultural and tolerant. The city opened its arms to the politically persecuted, as well as revolutionaries such as Karl Marx and Leo Trotsky, and granted asylum to refugees from Nazi Germany. It is a city that has always attracted artists and it is no coincidence that *major art movements* such as Impressionism and Cubism found their beginnings here. Painters like Auguste Renoir, Vincent van Gogh and Pablo Picasso as well as writers such as Voltaire, Victor Hugo, Honoré de Balzac, Charles Baudelaire, Marcel Proust, Ernest Hemingway and Jean-Paul Sartre lived and worked here. Artists met in cafés and brasseries that have since become famous on the left of the Seine – the *rive gauche.* This area, around the university buildings of the Sorbonne, has long been the *intellectual heart* of the city. The majority of these meeting places such as Café de Flore, or the existentialists' rendezvous Les Deux Magots in Saint-Germain-des-Prés, and the Closerie des Lilas in the former artists' district of Montparnasse, still exist today. These cafés and restaurants are a welcome place to stop by, especially for tourists and the well-heeled. But they, like the rest of the affluent metropolis, have long since become too expensive for poor poets and struggling artists.

Paris is multicultural and tolerant

Paris, with its capricious beauty, was home to all sectors of society for centuries, but it is now increasingly becoming a capital for the rich. A cappuccino can easily cost more than 5 euros, an evening meal served with wine, 60 euros or more. A statutory *cap on rents* introduced in 2015 is intended, at the very least, to make housing more affordable. However, the law does nothing to improve the poor condition of many residential buildings. The extravagantly ornate palace façades often conceal shabby backstairs and cramped attic rooms. These *chambres des bonnes*, the former servants' quarters, are now rented out to students and the less well off. In an effort to improve the housing situation and avoid further ghettoization, the city is now purchasing real estate in upscale districts in the city centre in order to renovate them and convert them into *subsidised housing*. It's a small ray of hope for Parisians in their fight against high prices, congested roads, air pollution, overcrowded public transport systems and crime – nearly everyone in Paris has experienced a burglary at some point.

But despite all these issues, the majority of Parisians are also a bit proud of their city. Their confidence is likely a result of the fact that in the past, Paris constantly had to reinvent itself. Today, too, ambitious projects are in the works, intended to make the city more liveable. The latest major project is entitled *Le Grand Paris*. The city of museums had grown too cramped and decided to open its arms to the surrounding suburbs, which were incorporated into the city. Paris is now building on what Napoleon III began in 1860, with the incorporation of Montmartre, Belleville and nine other communities: On 1 January 2016, Paris and 130 neighbouring communities merged to form the Métropole du Grand Paris, which is home to more than 7 million people. Important *infrastructure packages* have been passed in an effort to mitigate the chaotic traffic that often throttles the city streets. By 2030, four additional Métro lines are set to

The Eiffel Tower: 300-metre-high steel trelliswork and a world-famous Paris landmark

be added to the existing 14 to connect Paris to the surrounding communities. At that point, you will be able to travel to the two Paris airports, Roissy-Charles-de-Gaulle and Orly, by Métro. The hope is that upgrading the public transport system, implementing traffic calming measures, and adding new green spaces and recreational areas – such as along the Seine, where an urban highway was still active until recently – will reduce the pervasive

Major project: Paris becomes the Métropole du Grand Paris

road congestion. There is currently a flurry of construction activity in the high-rise district of *La Défense,* and skyscrapers are also going up along the city's inner ring road – much to the dismay of many Parisians. The city's stated goal is to defend its rank as a global capital against megacities like London, Tokyo, and New York.

WHAT'S HOT

1 Freshly roasted

Coffee France is rediscovering coffee thanks to the growing popularity of coffee shops that roast their own beans among young Parisians. Courses and tastings akin to wine seminars are even offered at *Caféotheque (52, rue de l'Hôtel de Ville | www.lacafeotheque.com)*. The coffee is also freshly roasted at *Café Lomi (3, rue Marcadet | cafelomi.com)*. Snacks such as banana bread and select cheeses are the perfect accompaniment to the *grand crus*. The stylish café *Coutume (47, rue de Babylone)* also stocks a huge selection of coffees.

Art to go

2

Spontaneous creativity Spontaneity can be ultra hip. Websites such as *www.la-boutique-ephemere. com* announce last-minute art and design sales at spontaneously determined places within Paris. *Art éphémèmere,* i.e. street art or murals on buildings, is particularly popular. The often witty stencil art *(pochoirs)* on the streets of Paris is always worth a second look. An overview of these popular art genres can be found at *www.trompe-l-oeil.info* or *urbanart-paris.fr*.

3 Your very own scent

Perfume An increasing number of French women are emphasizing their individuality by creating their own perfumes. In special ateliers *(www.abcduparfum.fr or www. cinquiemesens.com)*, you can learn the secrets that go into making a fine Eau de Toilette. After a three hour course in perfume and scents course, you'll go home with your very own signature scent.

Veggietown

Meat-free eating "What do you mean, you don't eat meat?" The waiter looks absolutely baffled. Until quite recently, it could be difficult to find vegetarian options in Parisian restaurants. But vegetarianism is on the rise here, as well. There are growing numbers of hip restaurants with vegetarian or vegan menu items, especially in the trendy districts north of the Seine. Around *Rue du Faubourg Poissonnière* and *Rue de Paradis* on the border between the 9th and 10th arrondissements, the selection of vegetarian dining options is so enormous that the *Association végétarienne de France (www. vegetarisme.fr)*, the French vegetarian association, dubbed this area the "Veggietown" of Paris. The days when vegetarians had to settle for a boring salad at Parisian restaurants are a thing of the past!

4

Virtual reality

Digital living Paris has a new dimension: The cinema chain *MK2* opened the city's first *virtual reality experience room (admission 12 euros/20 min., 24 euros/50 min. | 160, Av. de France | www.mk2vr. com)* in the southeast of the city. You can test out the latest VR productions at twelve stations. Space is limited, so reservations are a must. The content varies and covers all genres, from motion simulators and video games to short documentaries and feature films. Just put your headset on, and you're good to go! There was one stand-out hit at the launch: "Birdly", a flight simulator that allows you to slip into the feathers of a bird and take to the skies – virtually, of course.

5

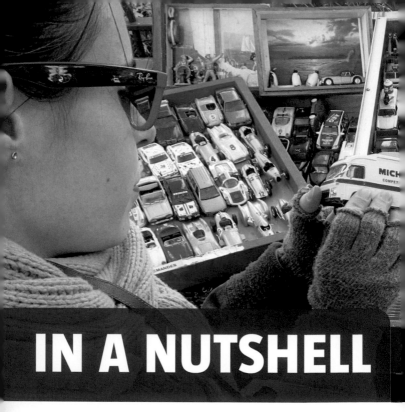

IN A NUTSHELL

BERLIN BUZZ

Frederick the Great once said that he would never have the foolish arrogance to presume Berlin could one day compare to Paris. Well, he was wrong! Today, young Parisians are pushing back against the historical weightiness of their city. They come back from Berlin buzzing with ideas and try to breathe some of the German capital's creative spark into Paris. They spontaneously occupy abandoned industrial sites before new building begins; the media hypes these new creative spaces as hip locations 'á la berlinoise'. Even without much publicity, word of a new hot spot spreads like wildfire on social networks. Rather than hopping on the next plane to Berlin, Paris's cool crowd has started meeting at run-down freight yards with graffiti and food trucks.

ON SET IN PARIS

Paris and the cinema have a long, shared history: It all started in 1895 with the first public film screening by the Brothers Lumière. Since then, Paris has been immortalised in countless films. Around 900 film shoots take place in the city every year. You've probably heard of films like "Amélie", Woody Allen's "Midnight in Paris" and "Untouchable". If you're interested in retracing the footsteps of film history in the city, contact Juliette Dubois from *Ciné-Balade (www.cine-balade.com)*. This cinema expert can regale you with countless anecdotes – in English – about the

Fluctuat nec mergitur: She is tossed by the waves but doesn't sink – true to their motto, the Parisians always stay calm

world of cinema in Paris. If you want to explore on your own, a collection of locations that have made their mark on film history is available on the website *Paris fait son cinéma (www.parisfaitsoncinema.com)*.

THIRSTY?

Many things are more expensive in Paris than they are elsewhere. But there's one thing you can have as much of as you want, completely free of charge: water. Parisians are proud of their high-quality tap water. At a restaurant, you can order a carafe of tap water *(carafe d'eau)* for free with your meal; it's a common practice in Paris. When you're on the go, you'll find public drinking fountains in many places. The most famous of them are the *Fontaine Wallace:* four graces carrying a dome decorated with dolphins. And yes: You can actually drink the water flowing through the middle. Why "Wallace?" Because after the Franco-Prussian War in 1872, the fountains were commissioned and donated to the city by an Englishman named Richard Wallace. Today, more than one hundred of these green, cast-iron, Renaissance-style fountains are still in operation throughout Paris. In parks and outside public toilets, too, you will find taps providing potable water. Recently, seven drinking fountains that produce INSIDER TIP carbonated water *(eau pétillante)* have been added around town. Yes, you read that right: free sparkling water for everyone! You can find the addresses of all the drinking fountains on *www.eaudeparis.fr/ carte-des-fontaines*.

LES PUCES

Paris' flea markets, especially the *Marché aux Puces de Saint-Ouen* (see p. 77) at the Porte de Clignancourt, are a major attraction in the metropolis. Every year, more than five million people visit the largest antique market in the world. In, and in front of, the many multi-level halls you can choose between clothing, various odds-and-ends and even a huge range of furniture. Every hall has its own theme – from Art Nouveau to the Seventies. For a number of years now, business has been floundering – because of the financial crisis and competition from internet vendors. Many vendors have given up entirely. For tourists, however, it's still a treat to wander around the various stands outside or through the halls, with the hope of finding a few bargains. Despite discussions about the future of flea markets there have also been some interesting new developments. In some of the halls, restaurants have become established, some even with jazz music. And once a year, the *Jazz Musette Festival* is taking place *(www. festivaldespuces.com)*.

MÉTRO STATIONS

Although it is not the oldest underground railway system in the world (it first opened in 1900), it is certainly one of the most densely knit networks. There is supposedly nowhere in Paris further than 1,900 feet from one of the 300 stations. After all, Paris would not be Paris without he famous wrought iron Art Nouveau Métro entrances by the artist Hector Guimard (1867–1942).

The arabesque-shaped *bouche du metro* (mouth of the Métro) at the station *Porte Dauphine* is particularly eye-catching with its flowers in the form of red lamps that grow out of the vine-like ironwork. The modern counterpart to the some 80 Guimard entrances is the glass masterpiece *kiosque des noctambules*, the night owls' pavilion, created by Jean-Michel Othoniel. It graces the entrance to the station *Palais Royal-Musée de Louvre* on the square in front of the Comedie Française with its colourful spheres of murano glass. Tastefully illuminated statues point the way to the largest museum in the world underground at the Louvre station. The *Arts et Metier* station, clad entirely in copper with huge cogwheels echoing the days of steam engines, is considered one of the most beautiful in the city. A wall mural at the *Bastille* station commemorates the mercurial history of the site. The *Cluny-Sorbonne* station has been embellished with beautiful mosaics by Jean René Bazaine, and its ceiling bears the names of famous former students of the nearby university.

PARIS WITHOUT A CAR

Paris is choked to death by the traffic. The Boulevard Périphérique is not the only ring road notorious for traffic jams. Inner city roads are also susceptible to gridlocks. Whenever the hot air balloon

Trees made of wrought iron: The art nouveau-style entrance to the Saint-Michel Métro station

over the Parc Citroën changes its colour to red, the air in the metropolis has become so dirty that it can be a danger to health. It is therefore no surprise that the mayor, Anne Hidalgo, wants to ban car traffic from the city centre as much as possible. Step-by-step, the four central districts are supposed to become strictly controlled traffic areas, and vehicles with diesel motors are to be banned completely by 2020. A viable alternative to a car is the bike rental system *Velib* (see p. 125). For longer distances, many Parisians favour the small electric cars of the *Autolib (www.autolib.com)* system. In and around Paris, it has more than 3,800 cars that can be rented at 1,000 different stations.

Certain streets and districts are closed to car traffic on Sundays, which helps reduce air pollution. And thanks to a 2015 citizens' initiative, the city even introduced one completely car-free day per year (www.parissansvoiture.fr). A 2.3 km (1.4 mile) stretch along the left Seine bank between the *Musée du Quai Branly* and the *Musée d'Orsay* has banned cars entirely. Today, it is lined with floating gardens, bars, restaurants, kids' activities, lounge chairs, and free fitness courses all year round. The closure of a further section of the motorways on the right bank of the Seine since autumn 2016

cafés within a matter of days after the attacks. And in a show of solidarity, visiting globetrotters joined them. Enjoying a meal or a glass of wine outdoors became a statement, an affirmation of the values of the French Republic: liberty, equality, and fraternity. As the restaurants and cafés affected by the attacks slowly reopened, UN Secretary General Ban Ki-moon himself stopped by to have a cup of coffee with the mayor of Paris. And it didn't take long before crowds were back to rocking out at the *Le Bataclan* concert hall (see p. 88). Naturally, the strictest security measures are in place. 'Plan Vi-

The Parisian lifestyle: A relaxing picnic lunch at Place des Vosges

has caused jubilation among nearby residents and grumbling among motorists.

PARIS IS STILL A FEAST

Paris is known for its packed cafés, restaurants and concert halls. After the terrorist attacks of 13 November 2015, you might think those places would be abandoned – but quite the opposite is the case. They're busier than ever! With grim determination, many Parisians returned to the terraces of their favourite

gipirate' is the name of the action plan drawn up by the French government; its aim is to prevent future terrorist attacks. In concrete terms, it means bag searches and a heightened police, military and security presence. Visiting some bars is like going through airport security – you're searched before you can enter, and you have to empty your water bottle. But that will only happen after you've stood in line for hours, because – you guessed it – Paris has kept on partying. Seeing soldiers armed with machine guns might make you feel uneasy, but you can dance that feeling away in no time.

PARIS INTERNATIONAL

You couldn't afford the cost of a trip around the world, so you opted for a city break in Paris instead? Not a bad choice – after all, you can experience the entire world here, condensed into about 100 square kilometres (39 square miles). If Parisians want to experience India, they head to *Passage Brady,* where they'll find rows upon rows of Indian restaurants. Here and on Rue du Faubourg Saint-Denis between Gare du Nord and La Chapelle, you'll find every souvenir you could have possibly brought back from a trip to India. *Rue Saint-Anne* may still be named after a French queen, but it has been firmly under Japanese control for years. *Chinatown*, on the other hand, is located in the 13th arrondissement, and if you exit the Métro at *Château Rouge,* you'll find yourself in the midst of a colourful, bustling African street market.

PICNIC

Parisians enjoy sitting outdoors. But in the light of increasingly high costs many residents and tourists have discovered the simple pleasure of a picnic at the appearance of the first rays of sunshine. A favourite spot is the pedestrian bridge, *Pont des Arts*, which has a view towards the Louvre and Île de la Cité and, on warm evenings, there is rarely enough space. The same holds true for the parks around the Eiffel Tower.

The sunlit quays on the Seine are even more popular, especially in the afternoon. A unique vista is the shadowy western tip of the island, *Île de la Cité*, especially at dusk, although it is usually crowded at this time. The romantically inclined and dance freaks often picnic on the Seine quay, *Saint-Bernard*, (left of the Seine, between Île de la Cité and Austerlitz station). Salsa and tango dancing are popular in the early evening around the small inlets directly on the river (free).

In the afternoon and late into the evening, picnicking can also be recommended along the ● INSIDER TIP *Canal Saint-Martin*. Picnickers spread out their blankets late in the evening along the romantic, tree-lined waterways with its quaint bridges and locks as they eat baguettes, cheese, pasties and quiches washed down with cider, wine or beer. A little further north, on the *Canal de l'Ourcq*, people don't only eat, but play boule and its scandinavian pendant, Mölkky. An economical and convivial affair in a typically Parisian atmosphere.

ORGANICALLY BEAUTIFUL

France has long lagged behind other countries in terms of environmental awareness. Now it's playing catch-up. Paris is in the grips of organic fever – the supermarket chain *bio c' bon (www.bio-c-bon.eu)* alone has opened more than 50 branches in the French capital over the last few years. The city's northeast is home to the "Bourgeois-Bohème" (Bobo for short), who live with their families in former factories converted into loft apartments, and their younger brothers, the hipsters, who zip through the city on their fixies. A new organic spot opens here nearly every week. For everything from cosmetics *(www.mademoiselle-bio.com)* and fashion *(www.ekyog.com)* to fast food *(www.bioburger.fr),* customers' main concern is that it's organic. You can find hundreds of listings for Paris's burgeoning organic scene on the website "Paris so Biotiful – le green city Guide" *(parisobiotiful.com).*

SIGHTSEEING

Whether you're set on visiting the major attractions, on the lookout for the most spectacular squares and expensive shops, or seeking the charm of "old Paris" with its winding lanes, what you make of your stay in Paris is entirely up to you.

In order to provide a better overview, the inner city has been categorised into five areas in this guidebook. Just pick the spots that interest you, and off you go!

To prevent your exploration of the city from becoming too much, it's well worth taking a break and seeking out one of the magnificent parks or relaxing in one of the numerous cafés to get a real feel for the Parisian way of life. People-watching is often an activity in itself. If you're tired of walking, the bus route 73 will take you past La Défense and the

CITY WHERE TO START?
Paris is large, and there is no so-called city centre. For a proper overview, it's best to take the Métro line M 2 to **Anvers (141 D5)** *(Ⓜ L4)*. As soon as the train is above ground, you'll see Sacré-Cœur. Once you've scaled the steps, you'll have Paris at your feet. For a close-up of the Île de la Cité and the Louvre the (admittedly complex) Métro/RER railway station **Châtelet-Les Halles (147 D–E5)** *(Ⓜ M8)* is the ideal starting point.

Superlative sites and smaller treasures to discover: Paris has much more to offer than the Eiffel Tower, the Louvre and Notre-Dame

Arc de Triomphe, down the Champs-Elysées and around the Place de la Concorde up to the Musée d'Orsay, and passes an array of sights on the way: an economical and comfortable means of taking in the city. Another possibility: grab yourself a rental bike from the nearest *Vélib' station* (see p. 125).

Paris is a city of museums, with more than 150 in total. So you'll have to accept that it's impossible to visit every one, and decide in advance which ones are for you. Anyone who capitulates in the face of the sometimes very extensive collections – in the Louvre, you would have to walk some 17 km (10½ miles) to see everything – can visit one of the many smaller city palaces which are often veritable treasure troves. Note that most of the city's museums are closed on Mondays, while many national museums are closed on Tuesdays.

The "Paris Museum Pass" *(www.parismuseumpass.com)* allows you to visit more than 50 museums and other places of interest (two days: 48 euros,

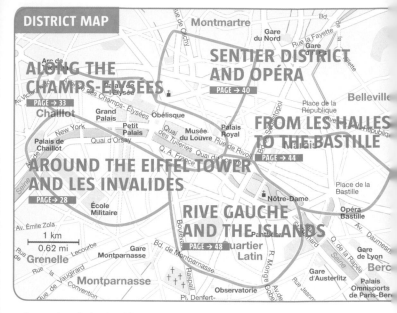

The map shows the location of the most interesting districts. There is a detailed map of each district on which each of the sights described is numbered.

four days: 62 euros, six days: 74 euros). You can obtain the pass at the Office du Tourisme (see p. 126), in Fnac stores as well as in many of the participating museums or simply online.

Incidentally, many museums are free on the first Sunday of the month. Most places offer discounts for students and senior citizens – EU passport holders under 26, for example, have free admission to all national museums *(musées nationaux)* in the city. Sometimes you can even skip the queue at the pay desk by showing your ID right at the entrance. Ask about that when you're there!

AROUND THE EIFFEL TOWER AND LES INVALIDES

The west of Paris (Paris Ouest) has long been the area preferred by the wealthier classes. The 16th arrondissement on the other side of the Seine and the 7th arrondissement between the Eiffel Tower and Les Invalides are among the most exclusive addresses in the city.

The elegant streets with consulates, ministries and several beautiful palaces are relatively calm and the pace more leisurely. Tourists crowd around this area to see the Eiffel Tower, the city's major landmark. INSIDER TIP The most popular photo opportunity, however, is on the other side of the Seine, from the vestibule of the Palais de Chaillot, whose side wings accommodate three museums and a theatre *(www.theatre-chaillot.fr)*. The most popular museum there is the *Cité de l'Architecture et du Patrimoine (www.citedelarchitecture.fr)*, in which the work of prominent French architects and their buildings from the 12th century onwards are exhibited.

You can INSIDER TIP avoid the lengthy queue in front of the Eiffel tower by booking with *Paris City Vision (www.pariscityvision.com)*. Or make a reservation (weeks in advance!) at one of the restaurants in the tower and enjoy the privilege of a private lift. You have a choice between *Jules Verne (daily | tel.01 45 55 61 44 | www.lejulesverne-*

paris.com | Expensive) or the less pricey *58 Tour Eiffel (daily | tel. 0145 55 20 04 | www.restaurants-toureiffel.com | Moderate–Expensive)* on the first floor. And if you don't want to either wait or dine, take a look at the tower from below and stroll through the nearby park to the end of the Esplanade des Invalides where Napoleon's tomb resides in Les Invalides.

🔲 EIFFEL TOWER (TOUR EIFFEL) ★
☀ (144 B5) (𝑚 F8)

Paris would not be Paris without the Eiffel Tower. The 300 m high (985 ft) landmark long held the distinction as the highest structure in the world. Built by Gustave Eiffel on the occasion of the 100-year anniversary of the French Revolution and the World Exposition in 1889, the steel structure was initially highly controversial. The tower was originally only meant to stay there for 20 years. But, because of its importance as a

MARCO POLO HIGHLIGHTS

weather station and later for air traffic as well as a radio and television station, it was allowed to remain.

The second platform, at a height of 115 m (380 ft), provides an impressive panoramic view over Paris; from the highest level at 274 m (900 ft), the view on a clear day extends right across the whole Paris basin. If you would like, you can INSIDERTIP sip a glass of champagne on the platform (from 13 euros). In 2017/2018, glass walls were installed around the Eiffel Tower to prevent terrorist attacks. *Daily 9.30am–11.45pm (lift) and 6.30pm (stairs), mid-June–early Sept 9.30am–12.45am (lift and stairs) | lift/stairs to 2nd floor 16/10 euros, 3rd floor 25/19 euros | 5, av. Gustave Eiffel | 7th arr. | RER C Champ de Mars – Tour Eiffel | www.toureiffel.paris*

2 INVALIDES (145 E5–6) (*G–H8*)

The *Hôtel des Invalides* is, after the palace at Versailles, the second largest building complex constructed during the reign of Louis XIV. The "Sun King" had it erected for his wounded war veterans. In order to prevent the ex-soldiers from becoming beggars or thieves, he set up special workshops governed by strict discipline to provide up to 3,000 invalids with work and good care. In addition to the soldiers' church, the Baroque *Dôme des Invalides* with its shining golden cupola is the main attraction. *Napoleon's tomb* reigns over the area beneath the dome. The annexed *Army Museum*, founded in 1794, is one of the largest of its kind in the world and testifies to the glory of the French Army. *Daily, April–Oct 10am–6pm, Nov–March 10am–5pm (April–Sept Tue until 9pm) | admission 11–12 euros |*

Les Invalides is the site of Napoleon's tomb which consists of six interlocking coffins

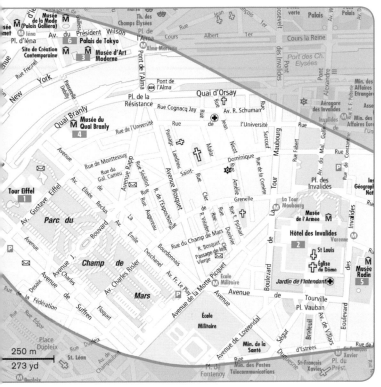

SIGHTSEEING AROUND THE EIFFEL TOWER & LES INVALIDES ▨ Pedestrian precinct

1 Tour Eiffel **4** Musée du Quai Branly – **6** Palais de Tokyo
2 Invalides Jacques Chirac
3 Musée d'Art Moderne **5** Musée Rodin

Esplanade des Invalides | 7th arr. | M 8 La Tour-Maubourg | M 13 Varenne | www.musee-armee.fr

▨ 3 MUSÉE D'ART MODERNE DE LA VILLE DE PARIS ● (144 C4) (*𝄞 F7*)
Among the exhibits of modern art (Fernand Léger, Robert Delaunay, Pablo Picasso, Georges Braque and Amedeo Modigliani), you can admire Raoul Dufy's *La Fée Electricité* and *La Danse* by Henri Matisse. The entrance area, book shop, and restaurant are being remodelled in 2018/2019. The museum will remain open. The entrance to the building will be temporarily moved to Quai de New-York. *Tue–Sun 10am–6pm (Thu temporary exhibitions until 10pm) | free admission (temporary exhibitions 5–12 euros) | 11, av. du Président Wilson | 16th arr. | M 9 Iéna | www.mam.paris.fr*

Part of the bronze sculpture "The Gates of Hell" in the garden at the Musée Rodin

◼ MUSÉE DU QUAI BRANLY – JACQUES CHIRAC ● (144 C4) (*⟊ F7*)

Even from outside, this museum designed by architect Jean Nouvel looks quite impressive. The vertical garden created by botanist Patrick Blanc and consisting of 15,000 plants is especially remarkable. Inside, it provides an extensive overview of non-European art objects. The exhibitions are attractively displayed with numerous multimedia installations. Special events are also regularly held, e.g. theatre, dance and music. Recommended: the museum's restaurant *Les Ombres* (see p. 65). *Tue, Wed, Sun 11am–7pm, Thu, Fri, Sat 11am–9pm | admission 10–12 euros (free 1st Sun of the month) | 37, Quai Branly | 7th arr. | M 9 Iéna | RER C Pont de l'Alma | www.quaibranly.fr*

◼ MUSÉE RODIN (145 E–F6) (*⟊ H8*)

No less a luminary than the German poet Rainer Maria Rilke, who temporarily worked as Auguste Rodin's private secretary, persuaded him to settle in this grand city palace. In addition to famous works such as *The Kiss* or *The Cathedral*, some works by his gifted pupil and lover, Camille Claudel, can also be seen here. The adjoining sculpture park and café are a perfect place to relax, surrounded by art. *Tue–Sun 10am–5.45pm | admission 10 euros, park 4 euros (Oct–March 1st Sun of the month free) | 77, rue de Varenne | 7th arr. | M 13 Varenne | www.musee-rodin.fr*

◼ PALAIS DE TOKYO (144 C3) (*⟊ F7*)

Not a museum in the classical sense. Contemporary artists present their sometimes provocative and giant installations in temporary exhibitions within the halls constructed for the 1937 World Exposition right next to the Musée d'Art Moderne de la Ville de Paris (see p. 31). In 2017, a second trendy museum restaurant opened alongside *Monsieur Bleu*e:

Les Grands Verres. Wed–Mon noon–midnight | admission 12 euros | 13, av. du Président Wilson | 16th arr. | M 9 Iéna | www.palaisdetokyo.com

ALONG THE CHAMPS-ELYSÉES

The famed and prestigious Champs-Elysées is a part of a vista which begins at the small arch of the Carrousel du Louvre, continues to the middle arch of the Arc de Triomphe and then ends to the west at the giant, modern, Grande Arche de La Défense.
Traffic on the multiple-lane grand boulevard is hectic day and night. Pandemonium also rules among the masses of tourists who spill out onto the broad pavements every season. In the boutiques, some of which are open until midnight, and in the numerous cafés, the motto "see and be seen" prevails. In order to uphold the standard, the city authorities have adopted a policy limiting the number of cheap chain stores that are permitted to settle in this coveted area. The grand boulevard is intersected at the lower end by the Avenue Montaigne, one of the most expensive addresses when it comes to fashion. The glass palaces, the Grand and Petit Palais, erected in 1900 on the occasion of the World Exposition, are located in this section lined by luxuriant greenery, along with the Palais de la Découverte *(www.palais-decouverte.fr)* which now houses a science museum.
Don't forget to make a detour to the right of the Louvre in the direction of Pont Alexandre III. From this vantage point you can really appreciate the splendour so typical of the Napoleonic era and the Belle Époque, and it is not difficult to imagine why people flocked to the World Exposition from far and wide to admire the splendour of this city. If you're game for another round of sightseeing, cross the Place de la Concorde and stroll down the elegant rue Royale to the church of Sainte-Marie Madeleine (La Madeleine). If you would rather relax instead, catch your breath in the Jardin des Tuileries then make your way to the adjacent Louvre.

LOW BUDGET

Every Saturday from 8pm to 9pm, a free organ concert is held in ● *Notre-Dame* **(147 E6)** *(Ø M9)*. *www.musique-sacree-notredameparis.fr*

What will you find at the *Musée de la Sculpture en Plein Air (Quai Saint-Bernard | 5th arr.)* **(154 A2)** *(Ø N9–10)* in the little *Jardin Tino-Rossi* on the banks of the Seine? An outdoor sculpture garden, completely free of charge! Here, you can stroll past 30 works by sculptors like César Baldaccini and Constantin Brancusi.

There are also sights you can visit for free, either on certain days or all year round. This website will let you know which days you can check out certain historical buildings and museums without having to pay: *en.parisinfo.com/discovering-paris/themed-guides/paris-for-free/free-museums-and-monuments-in-paris/free-admission-and-good-deals-in-museums-and-monuments-in-paris.*

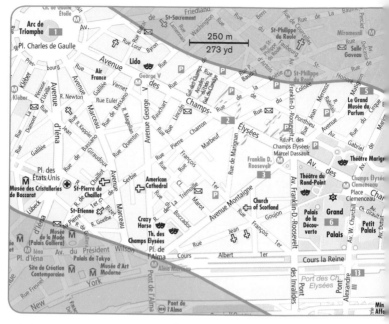

SIGHTSEEING ALONG THE CHAMPS-ÉLYSÉES

1 Arc de Triomphe
2 Avenue des Champs-Elysées
3 Avenue Montaigne
4 Carrousel du Louvre
5 Le Grand Musée du Parfum
6 Grand & Petit Palais
7 Jardin des Tuileries
8 Jeu de Paume
9 Musée du Louvre
10 Musée de l'Orangerie

Pedestrian precinct
11 Musée d'Orsay
12 Place de la Concorde
13 Pont Alexandre III

1 ARC DE TRIOMPHE ★
(144 B–C1) (*∅ F5*)

The 50 m high (165 ft) landmark created by Jean François Chalgrin, based on buildings from Antiquity, rises up along the impressive axis drawn between the small arch of the Louvre and the large arch of La Défense. After Napoleon commissioned the building in 1806 in honour of his "great army" and his victory at the Battle of Austerlitz, it took another 30 years until it was finished. Under the arch, which features important reliefs, including "La Marseillaise",

you will find the *Tombe du Soldat Inconnu (tomb of the unknown soldier),* the starting point for the military parade held every year on 14 July.

An underground passage near the Métro station at the Place Charles de Gaulle-Étoile leads past a small museum on the history of the Arc de Triomphe and to the entrance to the ✂ viewing platform. You should by no means miss this phenomenal view: no less than a dozen avenues radiate out from the monument in the shape of a star. *Daily, April–Sept 10am–11pm,*

Oct–March 10am–10.30pm | 12 euros (Nov–March 1st Sun of the month free) | M 1, 2, 6 | RER A Charles de Gaulle-Etoile | www.arc-de-triomphe.monuments-nationaux.fr

▣ AVENUE DES CHAMPS-ELYSÉES
(144 C–F 2–3) (*𝄞 F–H 5–6*)

The allegedly most beautiful street in the world is not particularly appreciated by Parisians, which is why it is mostly

A short detour to the *Avenue de Marigny* leads you directly to the front of the Elysée Palace, the president's residence. Famous addresses on the mile-long grand boulevard are the elegant perfumery *Guérlain (no. 68)*, the renowned dance theatre *Le Lido de Paris (no. 116)*, as well as the exclusive boutique, *Louis Vuitton (no. 101)*. *M 1 George V | M 1, 9 Franklin D. Roosevelt | M 1, 13 Champs-Elysées-Clemenceau*

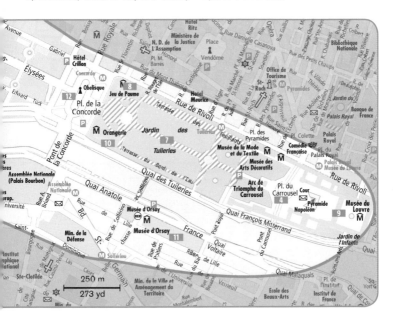

teeming with tourists between the Arc de Triomphe and Place de la Concorde. There are lengthy queues of tourists and locals alike in the evenings and especially at weekends in front of the large cinemas featuring premieres. While the upper part of the avenue consists of fast food chains and other ontemporary commercial outlets, the magnificence of the Belle Époque is more evident further down.

▣ AVENUE MONTAIGNE
(145 D3) (*𝄞 G6*)

The city's stretch of luxury boutiques, a side street of the Champs-Elysées, is where you'll find nearly every notable fashion designer (Versace, Ricci, Dior), jewellers, perfumeries and leather goods stores. It is not uncommon for customers to be brought to the entrance by their chauffeurs where they are then greeted by white-gloved porters. If you can afford to stay in a luxury hotel, try the *Plaza Athénée*. You will also find the *Théâtre des Champs-Elysées (no. 15)* with its beautiful façade designed by Antoine Bourdelle on this street. *8th arr. | M 1, 9 Franklin D. Roosevelt*

▨4 CARROUSEL DU LOUVRE ●
(146 C4) (*Ⓜ K8*)

The shopping arcade has only existed since 1990. The passages under the glass pyramid and the Louvre provide a venue for upscale shops as well as restaurants and cafés. This is the ideal place to take cover during a walk on a rainy Sunday or **INSIDER TIP**▸ to purchase last-minute gifts for friends and family back home. The *Boutique des Musées Nationaux* offers reproductions of works of art from various French museums plus a choice selection of cards and books. An eatery that offers a different style of refreshment after a long stroll: The *Restaurants du Monde (Budget)* serve specialities from all over the world. *Daily 8.30am–11pm | 1st arr. | M 1, 7 Palais Royal-Musée du Louvre | www.carrouseldulouvre.com*

▨5 LE GRAND MUSÉE DU PARFUM
(145 E2) (*Ⓜ H5–6*)

If you're feeling stuffed up, you might want to give this one a miss! This museum of perfumes opened in late 2016; you can smell over 70 different fragrances here, from the first perfume in history to the components of modern perfumes. *Tue–Sun 10.30am–7pm | admission 14.50 euros | 73, Rue du Faubourg Saint-Honoré | 8th arr. | M 9, 13 Miromesnil | www.grandmuseeduparfum.fr*

▨6 GRAND & PETIT PALAIS
(145 E3) (*Ⓜ H6*)

Both palaces were constructed for the 1900 World Exposition and their opulent and historicised decorative sculptures

symbolise one of the most flourishing cultural epochs of Paris. The iron and glass construction and domes are jewels of Art Nouveau and Belle Époque style. While the *Grand Palais (changing opening hours | 3, av. du Général Eisenhower | www.grandpalais.fr)* exclusively hosts first rate temporary exhibitions and will be closed for two years from 2020 due to renovations, the lavishly restored *Petit Palais (Tue–Sun 10am–6pm, Fri until 9pm | av. Winston Churchill | www.petitpalais.paris.fr)* has a permanent exhibition with artworks and paintings from the 18th and 19th centuries (free admission, temporary exhibitions 10–15 euros). *8th arr. | M 1, 13 Champs-Elysées-Clemenceau*

▨7 JARDIN DES TUILERIES
(146 A–B 3–4) (*Ⓜ J–K7*)

Regarded as the "front garden" of the Louvre, this Baroque park has existed

since 1666. It was one of the first parks opened to the general public and became a model for many other parks in Europe. Especially noteworthy are the 18 statues of women by Aristide Maillol, which seem almost surreal peeking out between the carefully manicured hedges.
1st arr. | M 1, 8, 12 Concorde | M 1 Tuileries

8 JEU DE PAUME
(146 A3) (*J6*)

Don't let the exterior fool you! This grand 19th-century gymnasium is anything but old-fashioned. Rotating exhibits bring 20th- and 21st-century imagery to life. You can also view photography, video and internet art in the museum's virtual gallery on its website: *espacevirtuel. jeudepaume.org. Tue 11am–9pm, Wed–Sun 11am–7pm | admission 10 euros | 1, Place de la Concorde | 8th arr. | M 1, 8, 12 Concorde | www.jeudepaume.org*

9 MUSÉE DU LOUVRE ★
(146 C4–5) (*K–L7*)

A well thought out strategy is required for a visit to the most sprawling museum in the world. After all, there is much more to admire in the Louvre than just the awe-inspiring ladies *Venus of Milo* (2nd century BC), Leonardo da Vinci's *Mona Lisa* (16th century) and Jan Vermeer's *The Lacemaker* (17th century). A very helpful map is available in English from the information desk, as is a weekly schedule of room closures. The free app 'My Visit to the Louvre' is also recommendable; it provides a 3D model and countless explanations of works of art to help you explore the 60,000 m2 (645,835 square feet) of gallery space. You can purchase an additional audio guide via the app for just under 5 euros. Culture seekers can then choose from a comprehensive range of exhibits

The park Jardin des Tuileries designed by André Le Nôtre is a World Heritage Site today

dating back to the 7th century B.C. that includes Oriental, Egyptian and Graeco-Roman civilisations divided among the three building complexes *(Denon, Sully, Richelieu)*. Alongside European sculpture from the Middle Ages to the 19th century, handicrafts and over 100,000 graphic art pieces spanning six centuries, the collection of paintings is quite a highlight. Sub-divided into regions, it documents European painting from the 13th to the 19th centuries. The exuberant stucco, the crown jewels and paintings by Charles Le Brun, Eugène Delacroix and others in the opulent *Apollon-Galerie* bear witness to the immense power of the Sun King, Louis XIV.

Take a break from your museum visit in the aesthetic underground shopping arcade, *Carrousel du Louvre* (see p. 36). Even if you forego a visit to the museum, it is still worthwhile to take a closer look at the Louvre complex, which was transformed from a 12th-century fortress into a Renaissance palace. The exposed *medieval foundations*, the beautifully illuminated *Cour Carée,* the small *triumphal arch* that forms a focal axis with its big brother and the audacious *glass pyramid* by the Chinese architect Ieoh Ming Pei are absolute highlights of any visit to Paris. The *Hall Napoléon* in the lobby below the Pyramid hosts special exhibitions.

Tickets are sold via the website or from the automatic ticket machines on site, which are easy to use. *Wed–Mon 9am–6pm (Wed and Fri until 9.45pm) | admission 15 euros (Oct–March 1st Sun of the month free) | M 1, 7 Palais Royal-Musée du Louvre | www.louvre.fr.*

🔟 MUSÉE DE L'ORANGERIE
(146 A4) (𝄞 J7)

The Jardin des Tuileries adjacent to the Louvre is home to the remarkable collection assembled by the art dealer Paul Guillaume, including works by Auguste Renoir, Pablo Picasso, Paul Cézanne, Henri Matisse and Amedeo Modigliani. The highlight is the famous *Nymphéas* (Water Lilies) by Claude Monet, whose eight large compositions adorn the walls in an elliptical form, enhancing the impression of flowing water and light.

TIME TO CHILL

Check out the *Bar à Sieste – Zzz-Zen* **(146 C3) (𝄞 K6)** *(Mon–Sat noon–8pm | 29, Passage Choiseul | 2nd arr. | tel. 01 71 60 81 55 | M 7, 14 Pyramides | www.barsieste.com)* in the nostalgic Choiseul shopping centre. In France, "Zen" always signals "relaxed". Without having to book ahead, you can relax on a Shiatsu massage lounger or chair and listen to ethereal music played through your headphones. The loungers are separated from each other by either walls or curtains. The most sophisticated Japanese devices knead and massage you for 25 to 45 minutes, depending on the programme you select. Prices range between 12 and 27 euros, which is not very much by Paris standards. A cup of organic tea is included. For a bit more pampering, head to the vaulted cellar for a fish pedicure (20 euros) or treat yourself to a manicure (from 12 euros).

Great art in an old railway station: sculptures in the central area of the Musée d'Orsay

A combined ticket with the Musée d'Orsay (16 euros) ensures priority in both queues. *Wed–Mon 9am–6pm | admission 9 euros (1st Sun of the month free) | Place de la Concorde | Jardin des Tuileries | 1st arr. | M 1, 8, 12 Concorde | www.musee-orangerie.fr*

⬛ MUSÉE D'ORSAY ★ ●
(146 A–B 4–5) (*🗺 J7*)

The painters of light, the Impressionists, form the focal point in the light-flooded rooms of this former railway station that was converted in 1986. Works by the precursors of modernist painting such as Vincent van Gogh, Paul Gauguin and Paul Cézanne can also be admired. The paintings, sculptures, collection of art objects as well as urban planning documentation, film and film poster art cover the period from 1848 to 1914, one of the most fruitful epochs in art history. Not only is the museum book shop's extensive selection impressive, but so is the elegant restaurant, where the modern seating harmonises well with the splendour of the Belle-Époque era. *Tue–Sun 9.30am–6pm (Thu until 9.45pm) | admission 12 euros (1st Sun of the month free) | 1, rue de la Légion d'Honneur | 7th arr. | RER C Musée d'Orsay | www.musee-orsay.fr*

🔢 PLACE DE LA CONCORDE
(146 A3) (*𝄞 J6–7*)

The most monumental square in Paris is superlative in every way: you have the entire Champs-Elysées up to the Arc de Triomphe before your very eyes from its centre point, the 3,300 year-old, 22 m high (75 ft) Egyptian obelisk. It is hard to imagine that, on this very square built in 1775, thousands of opponents of the Revolution – including Louis XVI himself and his wife, Marie-Antoinette, Robespierre and the Countess du Barry, met their deaths here by guillotine. The eight female statues framing the Place de la Concorde represent the eight largest cities in France. *8th arr. | M 1, 8, 12 Concorde*

🔢 PONT ALEXANDRE III
(145 E4) (*𝄞 H7*)

Tsar Nicholas II personally laid the foundation for the city's most magnificent bridge in 1896, which connects the Grand Palais and the Esplanade des Invalides. In sunny weather the gold of the winged Belle-Époque horses shimmering on the bridge's corner pillars can be seen from far and wide. *8th arr. | M 8, 13 | RER C Invalides*

SENTIER DISTRICT AND OPÉRA

The former Parisian cloth manufacturing district around the rue du Sentier is still the centre of haute couture sewing today, but on a smaller scale.

The pressure caused by cheaper imports from Asia has caused a number of businesses to close and even the wholesale trade is suffering from competition

The Pont Alexandre III is only one of 35 bridges over the Seine in Paris, but one of the prettiest

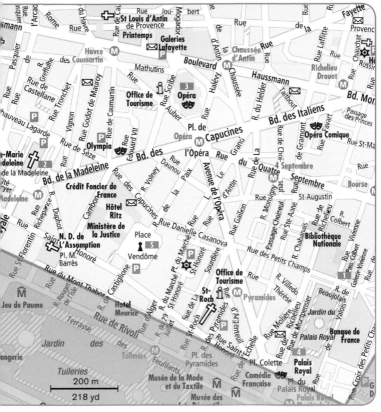

SIGHTSEEING IN THE SENTIER DISTRICT AND OPÉRA

▨▨ Pedestrian precinct

1 Galerie Vivienne

2 La Madeleine

3 Opéra Garnier

4 Palais Royal & Jardin du Palais Royal

5 Place Vendôme

from other regions. The chic Place des Victoires with boutiques and its architecturally stunning shopping arcades from the 19th century are a testimony to the former affluence of this district. You could easily spend half a day strolling through the covered shopping centres resplendent with mirrors, brass and wooden panelling, where you feel as if you have travelled back in time to the elegant 18th century (albeit slightly faded), when stagecoaches departed from here. The area between the Palais Royal and the Boulevard Montmartre is lined with some better and some less-well restored arcades, ideal for those looking for old books and handicrafts, or who enjoy shopping in exquisite, time-honoured

The Opéra Garnier was the largest opera house in the world when it was constructed in 1875

shops. Afterwards, enjoy a break in one of the area's quiet, stylish cafés. The famous department stores, Galeries Lafayette and Printemps, are also in the vicinity.

In this district of Paris a large amount of money is spent as well as earned. Apart from the imposing headquarters of major banks and insurance agencies there is also the classical building that houses the Paris stock exchange, although there has long been no floor trading here. The street cafés and restaurants are frequented by elegantly-clad business peo-

ple holding extended lunch meetings. The Opéra Garnier lends the district its share of culture. A little further north, the legendary artistic and entertainment district of Montmartre stretches up the hill (see Discovery Tour 2).

◼ GALERIE VIVIENNE ●
(146 C3) (*III L6*)

The gallery is considered the queen of Parisian arcades and was completely refurbished at the turn of the millennium. Here, under glass-domed roofs, you can saunter past select shops over the beautiful mosaics on the floor made in the neo-Classical style. After a visit to *Emilio Robba,* where you'll find the most gorgeous artificial flowers in the world, sample an exquisite *chocolat à l'ancienne* in the tea room, *A priori thé.* Not far afield is the building of the same vintage, the *Galerie Colbert* with its Pompeian-style rotunda. *4, rue des Petits Champs | 2nd arr. | M 3 Bourse*

2 ■ LA MADELEINE (146 A2) (*⑭ J6*)
Originally planned as a victory hall for the Grande Armée, this building was ultimately converted into a "modest" church after Napoleon's defeat in Russia. Today, Parisians come to the ostentatious *Sainte-Marie Madeleine* – which was modelled after ancient temples – not only to attend church services, but more often to take in one of the numerous classical concerts (admission around 30 euros, but many concerts are free of charge). *Daily 9.30am–7pm | Place de la Madeleine | 8th arr. | M 8, 12, 14 Madeleine | www.eglise-lamadeleine.com*

3 ■ OPÉRA GARNIER (146 B2) (*⑭ K5*)
The sumptuous palace laden with marble and gold was completed by Charles Garnier in 1875 and can (apart from opera and ballet performances) be visited outside rehearsal hours. The opulent vestibule is quite remarkable, as are the ceiling paintings created by Marc Chagall in 1964. *Daily 10am–4.30pm | 11 euros | Place de l'Opéra | 9th arr. | M 3, 7, 8 Opéra | RER A Auber | www.operadeparis.fr*

4 ■ PALAIS ROYAL & JARDIN DU PALAIS ROYAL (146 C3–4) (*⑭ K–L 6–7*)
A historic place of refuge in the turbulent city centre. Shaded by the lime trees, it was once an epicentre of historical significance. Cardinal Richelieu, who had the palace and its surrounding park constructed in 1634, later bequeathed it to Louis XIII. Its subsequent owners, the House of Orléans, expanded it. Behind the uniform façades with rounded, arched arcades, shops can still be found just like centuries ago. The French Revolution began here in July 1789. In the adjacent courtyard next to the *Comédie Française,* the columns of varying heights by Daniel Buren have provided an interesting counterbalance to the historical backdrop since 1986. *1st arr. | M 1, 7 Palais Royal-Musée du Louvre | www. domaine-palais-royal.fr*

5 ■ PLACE VENDÔME (146 B3) (*⑭ J–K6*)
This masterpiece of classical symmetry with its characteristic oblique square form on four sides was built at the end of the 17th century by the famous master builder

FIT IN THE CITY

The lovely *Parc des Buttes-Chaumont* (see p. 57) on the eastern side of the city with its bridges, pavilions and waterfalls is definitely worth the 15-minute Métro ride. And, if you want to do something to keep fit, arrive shortly before 9am for the free hour-long Qigong course offered by Maître Thoi, a master of this popular Chinese sport said to strengthen inner energy. For almost 25 years, Thoi has held his class 365 days a year, regardless of the weather, at Av. de la Cascade **(143 E5)** (*⑭ Q4*) across from the Rosa Bonheur restaurant *(M 7 Botzaris).*

Jules Hardouin-Mansart. A column in the style of a Roman Trojan column stands in the middle of the Place Vendôme, and at its crown Napoleon is depicted as a Roman emperor. Place Vendôme is also world-wide known for its renowned jewellers and the famous Hôtel Ritz, which benefits from the location's extraordinary atmosphere. *1st arr. | M 3, 7, 8 Opéra*

FROM LES HALLES TO THE BASTILLE

The new Forum des Halles *(forumdes halles.com)*, with its curved glass roof, opened its doors in 2016 in the "belly of Paris" (Émile Zola), where the indoor markets were once located. From here, it's just a stone's throw to the once-aristocratic Marais district.

This district begins right behind the world renowned cultural centre, the Centre Georges Pompidou. Many Jews have lived in this area since the beginning of the 12th century. The Shoah Memorial *(www.memorialdelashoha.org)* as well as the Jewish museum of art and history *(www.mahj.org)* are both located in Marais and document the Jews' turbulent fate in France. On Friday evenings there is always a hub of activity between the kosher shops and the few remaining synagogues. "Pletzl" on the rue des Rosiers has long been a gathering place for Jews from throughout Europe. Its small shops and restaurants are increasingly being replaced by trendy, upmarket stores.

Marais is not only a fashionable district but also the quartier of the gay community. Stores for men's cosmetics are interspersed with fancy women's clothing stores, jewellers, galleries and cafés where there is always something going on. The district's architecture is impos-

An artistic event both inside and out: the Centre Georges Pompidou

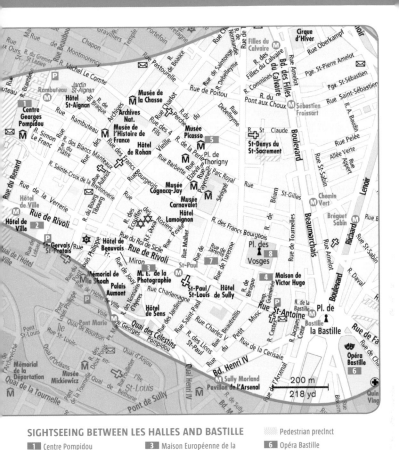

SIGHTSEEING BETWEEN LES HALLES AND BASTILLE

1 Centre Pompidou

2 Hôtel de Ville & Place de l'Hôtel de Ville

3 Maison Européenne de la Photographie

4 Maison Victor Hugo

5 Musée Picasso

6 Opéra Bastille

7 Place du Marché Sainte-Cathérine

8 Place des Vosges

Pedestrian precinct

ing with its many aristocratic residences, some of which house museums today. The Place des Vosges, a former royal square, is one of the most beautiful in Paris. Buskers play here year round. The centre of Paris' nightlife, just a short walk to the east of here, pulsates with activity until early morning in the shadow of the Opéra Bastille, around the rue du Faubourg Saint-Antoine, as well as further north in the vicinity of the rue Oberkampf.

1 CENTRE POMPIDOU ★
(147 E4) (∅ M7)

The fourth and fifth levels of this futuristic tubular structure give you a comprehensive overview of 20th-century art.

The interdisciplinary approach to graphic art, architecture, design and new media is fascinating. A true-to-life replica of the studio of the famous sculptor Constantin Brancusi is situated on the forecourt outside the building. ☼ On the sixth level, temporary exhibits of works by world renowned artists are displayed. The phenomenal view of Paris alone is worth a visit, which you can also admire from the designer café *Georges (restaurantgeorgesparis.com)*.

Next to the Centre is the fountain comprising water spraying sculptures by Niki de Saint Phalle and Jean Tinguely in a tribute to the ballet *Le Sacre du Printemps* by Igor Stravinsky, characterised by its colourful figures and technical contraptions. *Wed–Mon 11am–9pm (Thu temporary exhibitions until 11pm), Atelier Brancusi 2pm–6pm | admission 14 euros, observation deck 5 euros, Atelier Brancusi free (1st Sun of the month free) | Place Georges-Pompidou | M 11 Rambuteau | www.centrepompidou.fr*

② HÔTEL DE VILLE & PLACE DE L'HÔTEL DE VILLE (147 E5) (*M8*)

This has been the seat of Paris's city government since back in the middle ages. The current *city hall*, designed in neo-renaissance style, was constructed after the previous building was destroyed in an act of arson during the Paris Commune of 1871. Today, the only type of executions that take place in front of the building are verbal ones – the square is still a space for protests, as well as for fairs and sporting events. Parisians primarily flock to city hall to view the free rotating exhibits hosted here. For security reasons, tours are no longer being offered for the time being, but you can safely enjoy a virtual visit: *arts andculture.google.com/partner/mairie-de-paris. 4th arr. | M 1, 11 Hôtel de Ville*

③ MAISON EUROPÉENNE DE LA PHOTOGRAPHIE (147 F6) (*N8*)

This grand 18th-century villa is home to contemporary photography – rotating

The colourful Stravinsky fountain by Niki de Saint Phalle and Jean Tinguely

Bastille: a venue where people now storm in for the opera

exhibits of manageable size on a specific subject, movement or artist. Parisians attend the exhibits often and repeatedly. *Wed–Sun 11am–7.45pm | admission 9 euros | 5–7, rue de Fourcy | 4th arr. | M 1 Saint-Paul | www.mep-fr.org*

4 MAISON VICTOR HUGO
(148 B6) (*⑪ O8*)

The writer Victor Hugo lived and worked here between 1832 and 1848. Some of the ☆ rooms have an Asian influence. Here, you not only have a wonderful view of the Place des Vosges, but you can also marvel at the poet's documents, objects and paintings, which reveal he was also a very good painter – he left numerous paintings and around 3,000 drawings. *Tue–Sun 10am–6pm | free admission (temporary exhibitions 6–8 euros) | 6, pl. des Vosges | 4th arr. | M 1 Saint-Paul | www.maisonsvictorhugo.paris.fr*

5 MUSÉE PICASSO ★
(148 A5) (*⑪ N7*)

Some art aficionados claim that Pablo Picasso (1881–1973) was the greatest artist of the 20th century. The Picasso museum in Marais holds the largest col-

lection of his works with 5,000 pieces. After having closed for five years of renovations, the exhibition space has been expanded to over 39,000 square feet. Make sure to take a look at the artist's private collection with works by Henri Matisse, Edgar Degas, Paul Gauguin, Auguste Renoir and others. You will need plenty of time for this first rate museum and the stately *Hôtel Salé* in which it is housed. *Tue–Fri 10.30am–6pm, Sat/Sun 9.30am–6pm | admission 12.50 euros (1st Sun of the month free) | 5, rue de Thorigny | 3rd arr. | M 8 Saint-Sébastien-Froissart | www.museepicassoparis.fr*

6 OPÉRA BASTILLE
(154 B1) (*⑪ O9*)

The silvery façade of glass, steel and granite on the Place de la Bastille is hard to miss. The Canadian architect Carlos Ott constructed the new opera house in 1989. Even if you do not want to attend any of the opera or ballet performances, it is still worth the 1½-hour tour *(info on the website). Admission 15 euros | Place de la Bastille | 12th arr. | M 1, 5, 8 Bastille | www.operadeparis.fr*

7 PLACE DU MARCHÉ SAINTE-CATHÉRINE (148 A5–6) (*N8*)

The cafés and shady trees of this quiet location in Marais will carry you off to a tranquil marketplace in a provincial town in the South of France, especially in summer. *4th arr. | M 1 Saint-Paul*

8 PLACE DES VOSGES ⭐ (148 A–B 5–6) (*N–O8*)

At the beginning of the 17th century, King Henry IV commissioned the construction of the Place Royale. It is not only one of the oldest, but also one of the most architecturally harmonious squares in the city. The 36 pavilions (those for the king and queen are slightly higher) are framed by arcades where elegant art galleries and restaurants are now housed. Above these, the symmetrically arranged façades with their composition of light natural stone, red brick facing and grey slated roofs create a perfect picture. The uniformity of the ensemble is best appreciated from the small park situated in the centre of the square. *Marais | M 1 Saint-Paul, M 1, 5, 8 Bastille*

RIVE GAUCHE AND THE ISLANDS

The ⭐ Île de la Cité is the heart of Paris. The first inhabitants, the Parisii tribe, settled here during the Roman era.

This is also where the Gothic architectural masterpiece, the Cathédrale de Notre-Dame, is located. The fortified towers of the Conciergerie and the wonderfully light Sainte-Chapelle round off the medieval appearance of this vibrant area. On the neighbouring *Île Saint-Louis,* the pace is slightly more relaxed. This small island, which was long uninhabited, is now the most prestigious areas of Paris. The most lively street by far is the rue St-Louis, which has more ice cream shops than anywhere else in the city. In the summer, queues form from one to the next. The best place to enjoy your ice cream, is on the Pont Saint Louis, which connects both islands and where INSIDER TIP street musicians give their finest performances.

While the *rive droite* is traditionally more bourgeois, the Quartier Latin and Saint-Germain-des-Prés on the left bank of the Seine, the *rive gauche,* have long been the centres of intellectual life. Existentialists congregated in the cafés in the 1950s. Today these areas are fre-

Place des Vosges: fountains at the centre of a harmonious ensemble

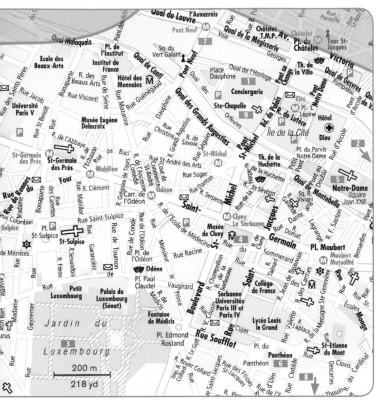

SIGHTSEEING ON THE RIVE GAUCHE AND THE ISLANDS　　　　▨ Pedestrian precinct

1 Conciergerie

2 Institut du Monde Arabe

3 Jardin du Luxembourg

4 Musée de Cluny

5 Notre-Dame

6 Panthéon

7 Pont Neuf

8 Rue Mouffetard

9 Sainte-Chapelle

quented predominantly by tourists and employees of the surrounding publishing houses and booksellers. The Quartier Latin (where Latin was once spoken) has housed the most famous educational institutions of the nation since the 13th century. In addition, the area has cafés and bistros as well as one of the most popular parks in Paris, the Jardin du Luxembourg.

1 CONCIERGERIE (147 D5–6) (Ⅲ L8)

The "antechamber to the guillotine" – as this former prison is rather grimly known – is an imposing structure on the Île de la Cité that chronicles a tragic episode in French history. The most prominent among the more than 2,000 inmates who faced their execution here were Marie Antoinette (her cell has now been reconstructed) as well as the revo-

More relevant than ever: the Institut du Monde Arabe

2 INSTITUT DU MONDE ARABE (153 F2) (🛍 N9)

The striking glass and aluminium façades, a successful paradigm of modern architecture by Jean Nouvel, follows the curve of the Seine. A gimmicky feature of the institute are the photography slats on the south side which open and close according to the fall of light. To promote the cultural exchange between the European and Islamic world, 20 Arab nations present forums, films and exhibitions, and there is also an extensive library. 🍽 The restaurant, *Le Zyriab,* provides a spectacular view over the roofs of the metropolis. *Tue–Fri 10am–6pm, Sat/Sun 10am–7pm | admission 8 euros | 1, rue des Fossés Saint-Bernard | 5th arr. | M 7, 10 Jussieu | www.imarabe.org*

3 JARDIN DU LUXEMBOURG ★ ● (152 B–C2) (🛍 K–L 9–10)

The most famous park in the centre of Paris is quite close to the Sorbonne. You can watch children sailing boats in the large pond from one of the available chairs. Maria de' Medici had the park and palace constructed at the beginning of the 17th century as an imitation of her native Florence. The *Palais du Luxembourg* is the headquarters of the French Senate today. The adjacent *Musée du Luxembourg (www.museeduluxembourg.fr)* often has exceptional art exhibitions. *Park: depending on the season 7.30/8.15am until 1 hour before sunset | 6th arr. | RER B Luxembourg*

4 MUSÉE DE CLUNY (153 D1) (🛍 L9)

The late Gothic city palace of the abbots of Cluny next to the Roman spas from the 3rd century provides the ideal setting for this display of medieval art. Apart from illuminated manuscripts, furniture, crafted pieces and ancient sculptures, the stained-glass windows

lutionaries Georges Danton and Maximilien de Robespierre. The picturesque building with its rounded towers was originally a palace of the Capetian ruling dynasty from the 10th century. The *Salle des Gens d'Armes* is considered one of the most impressive examples of Gothic secular architecture. Its name is derived from the word *concierge,* or chamberlain, who was accorded great power by the king from around 1300 onwards. *Daily 9.30am–6pm | admission 9 euros, incl. Sainte-Chapelle 15 euros (Nov–March 1st Dun of the month free) | 2, Blvd du Palais | 1st arr. | www.paris-conciergerie.fr*

and wall tapestries are especially stunning. The round salon featuring six wall tapestries of the *Lady with the Unicorn* (15th century) is a highlight. While the first five tapestries are allegories of the five senses, the meaning of the sixth is a mystery which holds every visitor under its spell. Please note: The museum will be periodically closed for phases of renovation until 2020. *Wed–Mon 9.15am–5.45pm | admission 8 euros (1st Sun of the month free) | 6, pl. Paul Painlevé | 5th arr. | M 10 Cluny-La Sorbonne | www.musee-moyenage.fr*

5 NOTRE-DAME ★ (147 E6) (⌖ M9)
This Gothic masterpiece was built between 1163 and 1345 at the instigation of Bishop Maurice de Sully. A Roman temple once stood on the square 2,000 years before. The interior of the five-aisled nave can accommodate 9,000 people. The three large entrance portals, the massive buttresses around the choir and the rose windows with a diameter of over 32 feet are especially impressive.

Many historically significant events have taken place here, including Napoleon's coronation. During the revolution, Notre-Dame was transformed into a "Temple of Reason" and the church seemed to be in danger of demise. In his book *The Hunchback of Notre-Dame,* Victor Hugo successfully appealed to the public to stop tolerating the situation, and the cathedral was restored as a result. The ⚡ tower provides a good view of the gargoyles as well as the city. In the forecourt there is

FOR BOOKWORMS & FILM BUFFS

Lost in Paris – Despite its title, this film starring comedic couple Dominique Abel and Fiona Gordon (also the directors) actually gives a good overview of the city! It's a poetic comedy: the story of a Canadian librarian who travels to Paris looking for her elderly aunt and meets a homeless Parisian man. The 2017 film takes viewers over and under Paris's bridges and shows both the beautiful and the dark sides of the city of lights.

Paris, Fenêtres sur l'Histoire – In his photo book, Parisian blogger Julien Knez carefully superimposed historical images of the city onto contemporary photographs. Embedded in today's Paris in this way, these photographic flashbacks give us a more palpable feeling for the city's history, from the Paris Commune of 1871 to May 1968 (2016).

Robert Doisneau – Through the Lens – Discover Paris by tracing the footsteps of photographer Robert Doisneau (1912–94). His world-famous black-and-white photographs still shape the way we think about the city. His photo of a kissing couple in front of Paris City Hall, for example, is legendary. In this 2016 documentary, the photographer's granddaughter Clémentine Deroudille profiles her grandfather's works.

750 Years in Paris – Don't worry, this isn't a weighty historical tome. On the contrary: it tells the story of Paris based on a single house, and without a single word. Parisian illustrator Vincent Mahé drew the same house 60 times, illustrating how it changed over the course of history, from 1265 to the attack on Charlie Hebdo in 2015. A journey through time, in pictures.

Notre-Dame: mythical creatures as figurative decoration high above the cathedral tower

a special marking from which distances to other French cities can be measured. *Mon–Fri 7.45am–6.45pm, Sat/Sun 7.45am–7.15pm | free admission | tower: April–Sept daily 10am–6.30pm, Oct–March daily 10am–5.30pm | admission 10 euros (Nov–March on the 1st Sun of the month free) | Parvis Notre-Dame-Place Jean-Paul II | Île de la Cité | M 4 Cité or St-Michel | RER B, C Saint-Michel-Notre-Dame | www.notredamedeparis.fr | www.tours-notre-dame-de-paris.fr*

⑥ PANTHÉON (153 D2) (∭ L10)

This massive domed structure can be seen from a distance on the hill of Sainte-Geneviève. Louis XV had the edifice constructed in 1756 by his master builder Jacques-Germain Soufflot as the fulfillment of a vow to Geneviève, the patron saint of Paris. Shortly after the Revolution, the church became the final resting place of French luminaries such as Voltaire and Jean-Jacques Rousseau. Since Victor Hugo's body was transferred to the Panthéon in 1885, this building – that is still occasionally used as a place of worship – was finally considered a mausoleum. You can also scale the stairs to the ⚜ gallery of the dome from which the physicist Léon Foucault conducted his famous pendulum experiment demonstrating the earth's rotational axis. *April–Sept daily 10am–6.30pm, Oct–March daily 10am–6pm | admission 9 euros (Nov–March 1st Sun of the month free) | Place du Panthéon | 5th arr. | M 10 Cardinal Lemoine | RER B Luxembourg | www.paris-pantheon.fr*

⑦ PONT NEUF (147 D5) (∭ L8)

The "new" bridge that crosses the top of the Île de la Cité is in fact the city's oldest existing bridge. When Henry IV, whose equestrian statue stands atop the structure, inaugurated the bridge in 1607, it was considered highly modern. For the first time in Paris, the view from a bridge of the Seine was unobstructed by houses. It is the most famous crossing point on the Seine – often sung about, the object of countless paintings and the backdrop for many films. The ░░░ `INSIDER TIP` square beneath the equestrian statue provides a magnificent view of the Louvre. *1st/6th arr. | M 7 Pont Neuf*

8 RUE MOUFFETARD
(153 E2–4) (*M10–11*)

This little street has wound its way down the vibrant Montagne Sainte-Geneviève since Roman times. Students from schools in the area, tourists and locals treasure the narrow street with its well-stocked market (Tue–Sun) at the lower end as well as its small bars and boutiques. The scenic *Place de la Contrescarpe* with its lovely cafés is located at the upper end of the "Mouff". *5th arr. | M 7 Place Monge*

9 SAINTE-CHAPELLE
(147 D6) (*L8*)

This veritable treasure chest of Gothic architecture lies virtually hidden in the courtyard of the central law courts on the Île de la Cité. The 13th-century church houses valuable relics from the Holy Land. The effect of the massive stained glass windows reaching for the heavens, held together only by filigree buttresses that bathe the entire room in a pale blue light is breathtaking. The upper floor is the actual chapel and was reserved for the king. *April–Sept daily 9am–7pm, Oct–March daily 9am–5pm | admission 10 euros, incl. Conciergerie 15 euros (Nov–March 1st Dun of the month free) | 8, bd. du Palais | 1st arr. | M 4 Saint-Michel or Cité | www.sainte-chapelle.fr*

OTHER DISTRICTS

BELLEVILLE
(148–149 C–D 1–2) (*P–Q 5–6*)

In contrast to the wealthy west of the city, the Belleville district has largely maintained its folksy charm. *Villa de l'Ermitage* and *Cité Leroy,* hidden alleyways lined with tiny houses, give us an idea of how 19th-century Parisian workers must have lived. You can still experience authentic local culture without all the tourist hype at a number of "musettes" in the area – almost like back in the days when Edith Piaf was growing up here; the small *Musée Edith Piaf (Mon–Wed 1pm–6pm, Thu 10am–noon / only after pre-booking by phone: tel. 0143555272 | free admission | 5, rue Crespin du Gast| 11th arr.)* displays various aspects of her life. Ever since artists discovered the charm and relatively low prices of the area, Belleville has become fashionable. Enjoy a beautiful view over Paris and the alleyways winding up the incline of ░░░ Belvedere from the upper half of Belleville park. *20th arr. | M 2, 11 Belleville*

BIBLIOTHÈQUE NATIONALE DE FRANCE
(154 C5) (*P12*)

Interested in modern architecture? Then head for the four glass towers shaped like open books surrounding a little copse near the banks of the Seine. Completed in 1996, the French National Library building was an initiative of President François Mitterrand. *Tue–Sat 10am–7pm/8pm, Sun 1pm–7pm | admission library 3.90 euros/day, free from 5pm, special exhibits 9 euros | Quai François Mauriac | 13th arr. | M 14, RER C Bibliothèque François Mitterrand | www.bnf.fr*

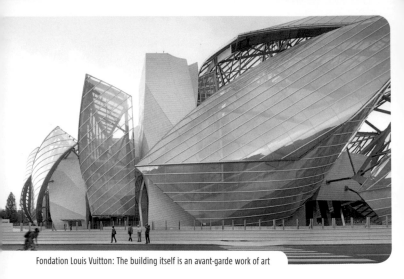

Fondation Louis Vuitton: The building itself is an avant-garde work of art

BOIS DE BOULOGNE
(136–137 B–E6) (🅜 A–D 4–9)

The large green lung to the west of Paris covering an area of over 3 square miles was the fashionable recreational meeting place at the beginning of the 20th century. The many hiking, riding and bicycle trails as well as small lakes, two horse-racing tracks and diverse restaurants are located in the park and its forests that have sadly been dissected by many roads and are the workplace of prostitutes. In the 18th century, the nobility built small summer residences. One of the most popular is the small castle of Bagatelle in the *Parc de Bagatelle (admission May–Oct 2.50 euros, Nov–April free)*, which is beautifully manicured and intersected by streams. The rose garden is a delight for flower lovers.

The nearby *Jardin d'Acclimatation* is a children's paradise (see p. 118) and an oasis in the big city also for grown-ups. There are two bicycle rental agencies and rowing boats for hire at the *Lac Inférieur*. *M 1 Les Sablons*

LES CATACOMBES ● (152 B5) (🅜 K12)

Stone was extracted from the underground quarries and used for Paris' buildings. The over 185-mile-long network of passageways, which some Parisians use for illegal parties, is partially open for tours. Since Parisian cemeteries were overcrowded until the 18th century, the bones of previous generations were decoratively piled up in these catacombs. *Tue–Sun 10am–8.30pm, last admission 7.30pm, often very long queue times! | admission 13 euros or 29 euros online at b12-gat.apps.paris.fr for admission and audioguide, without having to queue | start of tour: Place Denfert-Rochereau | 14th arr. | M 4, 6, RER B Denfert-Rochereau | www.catacombes.paris.fr*

CIMETIÈRE DE MONTMARTRE
(140 B3–4) (🅜 J–K3)

A number of artists and literati including Hector Berlioz, Heinrich Heine, Alexandre Dumas, Edgar Degas, Jacques Offenbach, François Truffaut, Vaslav Nijinsky, Emile Zola and Stendhal found their final resting place in this picturesque cemetery. *Daily 8/9am–5.30/6pm | 20, av. Rachel (main entrance) | 18th arr. | M 2 Blanche | M 2, 13 Place de Clichy*

CIMETIÈRE DU PÈRE LACHAISE ●
(149 E–F 4–5) (*Q–R 7–8*)

With an area of 110 acres, 12,000 trees, 1.5 million graves and ostentatious tombs, this cemetery is certainly the largest and most spectacular in Paris. In particular, the graves of the *Doors* lead singer Jim Morrison as well as Edith Piaf attract a huge following. Yves Montand, Baron Haussmann, Honoré de Balzac, Marcel Proust, Oscar Wilde, Frédéric Chopin and Molière are also buried here. *Daily 8/9am–5.30/6pm | main entrance: blvd. Ménilmontant | 20th arr. | M 2, 3 Père Lachaise | M 2 Philippe Auguste | www.perelachaise.com* (incl. virtual tour)

LE CORBUSIER

17 works by French-Swiss architect Le Corbusier were named World Heritage Sites in 2016. You can visit two of these buildings in Paris: the home of art collector Raoul La Roche and the studio and flat of the architect himself. Both buildings are located in the fashionable 16th arrondissement, about a 20-minute walk apart. *Admission 8 euros each, joint ticket 12 euros. Studio & apartment* (156 A4) (*B10*) *(2018 re-opening after renovations | 24, Rue Nungesser et Coli | M 10 Porte d'Auteuil)* and *Maison La Roche* (156 A4) (*B9*) *(Mon 1.30–6pm, Tue–Sat 10am–6pm | 10, Square du Docteur Blanche | M 9 Jasmin). www.fondationlecorbusier.fr*

FONDATION LOUIS VUITTON
(136 C6) (*B5*)

Since the end of 2014, a huge futuristic glass cloud designed by the famous architect Frank Gehry has graced the eastern part of Bois de Boulogne. The building with its slightly confusing galleries ranging in height from 11 m (36 ft) to 21 m (69 ft) is a masterpiece in itself. It houses recent pieces by internationally renowned artists, including Gerhard

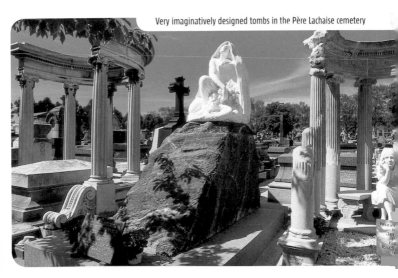

Very imaginatively designed tombs in the Père Lachaise cemetery

Richter, Jeff Koons and Olafur Eliasson. Temporary exhibitions as well as contemporary music concerts round out the offerings. *Changing opening times depending on the season | admission 16 euros | 8, av. du Mahatma Gandhi | M1 Le Sablons | www.fondationlouisvuitton.fr*

Portrait artists at work at the Place du Tertre

INSIDER TIP LA GAÎTÉ LYRIQUE
(147 E3) *(M6)*

Today, this former theatre built in the 19th century is a temple to digital culture. You can try out the latest video games for free at the eight gaming stations. Also on the docket: concerts, exhibitions, film screenings. *Tue–Sat 2pm–8pm, Sun 2pm–6pm | 3 bis, Rue Papin | 3th arr. | M 3, 4 Réaumur-Sébastopol | www.gaite-lyrique.net*

MONTPARNASSE
(152 A–B 3–4) *(J–K 10–12)*

The *Tour Montparnasse (April–Sept daily 9.30am–11.30pm, Oct–March Sun–Thu 9.30am–10.30pm, Fri/Sat until 11pm | 17 euros | www.tourmontparnasse56.com)* skyscraper that towers above everything else can only really be appreciated when standing on its viewing platform, the highest in Paris. When you wander through this district, you will find ugly buildings constructed in the 1960s alongside idyllic, green courtyards and studios once used by great artists and still used for artistic purposes today. Renowned artists such as Pablo Picasso, Amedeo Modigliani, Marc Chagall and Henri Matisse worked in the *Chemin du Montparnasse* on the Avenue du Maine after World War I. The places they frequented, namely La Coupole, Closerie des Lilas, Le Dôme or La Rotonde, are still favourite meeting places. Lenin and Leo Trotsky held political meetings in La Rotonde that were regularly interrupted by the police. Literary figures such as Samuel Beckett and Charles Baudelaire, the actors Jeanne Moreau and Philippe Noiret and the literary couple Jean-Paul Sartre and Simone de Beauvoir are buried at the *Cimetière du Montparnasse. 14th arr. | M 4, 6, 12, 13 Montparnasse-Bienvenüe | M 6 Edgar Quinet*

INSIDER TIP MUSÉE MARMOTTAN
(158 C4) *(C7)*

The painting that gave Impressionism its name, *Impression Soleil Levant*, hangs next to a hundred other masterpieces by Claude Monet (1840–1926) on the lower level of the opulent villa near the Bois de Boulogne. Precious biblical paintings as well as paintings from Monet's private collection (including works by Edgar Degas, Edouard Manet and Auguste Renoir) hang in the upper living area. A must for every lover of

Impressionist art! *Tue–Sun 10am–6pm (Thu until 9pm)* | *admission 11 euros* | *2, rue Louis Boilly* | *16th arr.* | *M 9 La Muette* | *www.marmottan.fr*

PARC DES BUTTES-CHAUMONT ⚜ (142–143 C–E 5–6) (*ⓜ P–Q 4–5*)

In the 19th century, Napoleon III had a picturesque landscaped park laid out in the English style with grottoes, rock formations, valleys, shrines and waterfalls on a waste tip in the then-notorious eastern part of Paris. With the help of the most modern technology of the day and numerous explosives, the terraced grounds were created to a variety of different designs – including one with a lake and an island – and planted with unusual vegetation. *19th arr.* | *M 7b Buttes-Chaumont*

PLACE DU TERTRE (141 D4) (*ⓜ L3*)

There is hardly a trace of the former village-like calm here. Instead, the area has been taken over by droves of tourists clamouring for their portrait rendered by artists of varying talent. The cafés that border the square are ideal for reminiscing about the era when luminaries of the arts still whiled away their time here. *M 12 Abesses*

SACRÉ-CŒUR (141 D4) (*ⓜ L3*)

The dazzling white basilica rising high above the city on Montmartre seems almost surreal, and cynics claim the domes look as if a confectioner has been having fun. The interior has a stunning giant golden Byzantine-style mosaic. The edifice was built as a national monument after France's defeat by Germany in the Franco-Prussian War of 1870/71. In 1919 the pilgrimage church was dedicated to the "Sacred Heart of Jesus". Today, thousands make the pilgrimage up the many steps and enjoy the impressive view over Paris from the ● ⚜ church's forecourt. A more comfortable option for making the ascent is a small mountain railway. *Daily 6am–11.30pm* | *35, rue du Chevalier de la Barre* | *8th arr.* | *M 13 Anvers* | *www.sacre-coeur-montmartre.com*

OUTSIDE THE CITY

SAINT-DENIS (158 C2) (*ⓜ 0*)

Stunning, early Gothic pillared basilica (begun in 1135) which became the prototype for this architectural style in France. A visit to the *royal tombs* is one of the highlights of any tour of this church located in the Paris suburb Saint-Denis. For centuries, nearly every ruler of the nation was buried here. There are 75 monumental tombs in the crypt, each guarded by life-sized statues of the deceased. The first church was built on this site in the 5th century when the martyr Denis allegedly walked up Montmartre with his severed head tucked under his arm. *Summer Mon–Sat 10am–6.15pm, Sun noon–6.15pm, winter Mon–Sat 10am–5.15pm, Sun noon–5.15pm* | *tombs: 9 euros* | *M 13 Basilique de Saint-Denis* | *www.saint-denis-basilique.fr*

SAINT-GERMAIN-EN-LAYE (158 A3) (*ⓜ 0*)

Excursions to the old royal city Saint-Germain-en-Laye were already popular among Parisians in the 19th century. This was not only on account of the convenient connection to the nation's first railway system which was constructed in 1837. French royalty resided in the town of 40,000 inhabitants until the end of the 17th century.

The landscape architects of Versailles laid out a beautiful *park* around the fortress-like, pentagonal *palace* with an over mile-long 🔭 *viewing platform* high above the Seine. Saint-Germain has retained the flair of a pleasant provincial town. The old town's streets and pedestrianised lanes with the beautiful palaces of the nobility and the large forest are ideal for a stroll and make an unforgettable outing. In addition, many shops are open on Sunday morning.

The *tourist office (38, rue au Pain | www.saintgermainenlaye-tourisme.fr)* is situated in the house where the composer Claude Debussy was born. The INSIDER TIP *studio of the Symbolist painter Maurice Denis (www.musee-mauricedenis.fr)* is worth a visit where works by Paul Gauguin and Pierre Bonnard are also exhibited. Saint-Germain-en-Laye is only 25 minutes away from Charles de Gaulle-Etoile via RER A.

VERSAILLES ★(158 B4) (*ɯ 0*)

A Paris stay is not complete without a visit to Louis XIV's gigantic palace. There is virtually nowhere else where the power of the monarch is so resolute and impressive, yet tastefully and harmoniously implemented as in Versailles. The absolutist and centralist concept of a nation was personified by the "Sun King", Louis XIV (1638–1715). At his behest, nearly all of France's nobility resided here, which meant that as many as 20,000 people had to be provided for as well as entertained with lavish celebrations.

Absolute must-sees during the tour of the *palace (April–Oct Tue–Sun 9am–6.30pm, Nov–March Tue–Sun 9am–5.30pm | admission 18 euros, Nov–March 1st Dun of the month free)* are the *royal chapel,* the *opéra* and the *state rooms* on the first floor, the walls of which are finished in marble and decorated with gold brocade. Don't miss the 245-foot-long *Hall of Mirrors*, whose 17 windows cast light onto the mirrors opposite.

Once measuring 23 square miles, the *park (April–Oct daily 8am–8.30pm, Nov–March daily 8am–6pm | admission free, except April–Oct Sat/Sun and sometimes Tue for the Grandes Eaux Musicales 9.50 euros)* still covers an area of 2,000 acres. During the *Grandes Eaux Musicales* classical music provides the background for the water displays in the fountains of the park. In addition to the pond where you can enjoy boat rides, highlights inlcude the two smaller castles *Grand* and *Petit Trianon*. The newly designed *Domaine de Marie-Antoinette et Grand Trianon (April–Oct Tue–Sun noon–6.30pm, Nov–March Tue–Sun noon–5.30pm | admission 12 euros)* includes grottoes, a temple of love and streams in the pretty English garden as well as *Le Hameau*, the idealised replica of a village farm complete with a pond.

If you prefer not to walk, you can cycle, take a tourist train or a boat ride. *Complete "Passport Château Versailles"* package *20 euros, 27 euros on the days of the Grandes Eaux Musicales*. Advance ticket sales on the Internet: *www.cha teauversailles.fr*.

The easiest and quickest way to reach Versailles from Paris is on the suburban train RER C (Versailles-Rive Gauche), which takes around 30 minutes. It is only a short walk from the railway station. Trains to Versailles-Rive Droite (then bus marked Phébus) travel every 15 minutes from the Gare Saint-Lazare and from the Gare Montparnasse (direction Chartres) to Versailles-Chantier (then bus marked Phébus). Bus route 171 goes from the Métro station Pont de Sèvres (M 9) to the palace.

A little tip: If you're travelling on single tickets, buy a return journey before you depart. That way, you won't have to waste time with tedious queueing in Versailles. Count on spending at least a day at Versailles and don't forget to wear comfortable shoes.

France's most famous palace and World Heritage Site: Versailles

FOOD & DRINK

To the French, eating is so much more than simply nourishment. It is also an essential means of social interaction and a vital ingredient in enhancing the quality of life.

If you want to discover the multifaceted gastronomy of France for yourself, which is well-represented in the top notch restaurants in the capital, you ought to know the fundamental aspects of French eating habits beforehand.

Breakfast *(petit déjeuner)* in France is modest by the standards of many other nations, but rightfully so: you'll need room for the much more substantial lunch *(déjeuner)*, that often lasts for two hours and is only half as costly as dinner *(diner)*.

Most restaurants do not open for dinner in the evening before 8pm. The French like to start their evening with an *apéritif* (*apéro* – kir, champagne or pastis, or simply a beer), accompanied by more or less sophisticated nibbles. You'll then be faced with the decision whether to order *à la carte* (from the menu) or *table d'hôte* (a set meal). The latter is better value for money if you are hungry, since a set meal traditionally consists of an appetiser *(entrée)*, main course *(plat)* – usually meat *(viande)* or fish *(poisson)*, cheese *(fromage)* and dessert. Dessert and cheese are frequently offered as alternatives. Tap water *(eau en carafe)* and bread *(pain)* are automatically provided with your meal. A *café* or *déca* (decaf-

Bon appétit: the French are no breakfast people, but they make up for it big time at lunchtime and in the evening

feinated coffee) should not be forgotten. An extensive wine list is the sign of a good restaurant. A tip *(pourboire)* of 5–10 percent is de rigueur.

BRASSERIES

Brasseries are very much part of the Paris scene. As opposed to a small, cosy bistro with a modest menu, brasseries are fairly large restaurants which sprang up at the turn of the 20th century and served hearty fare in addition to seafood specialities. Many brasseries hold the distinction as a protected historical site with their glamorous Belle-Époque décor. Though the food is not exactly cheap in these restaurants, it is still relatively affordable *(Moderate)*.

BOFINGER ● (148 B6) *(ᗰ O9)*

The *choucroute de la mer,* sauerkraut with fish and other seafood, is a hit, served in a striking Art Nouveau setting under a glass dome. *Daily | 5–7, rue de la Bastille | 4th arr. | tel. 0142 72 87 82 | M 1, 5, 8 Bastille | www.bofingerparis.com*

BRASSERIE LIPP (146 B6) (*M K8*)

Probably the most famous brasserie in Paris. Here, you'll find statesmen, writers, actors, and of course, hordes of tour-

JULIEN ⭐ (147 F2) (*M M6*)

Extravagant stucco, vine-covered Art Nouveau maidens, colourful glass ceilings with mirrored walls. As you're marvelling at the décor, don't forget about the food! It would be a pity to miss out on the delicious fish – a chef's speciality. *Daily | 16, rue du Faubourg Saint-Denis | 10th arr. | tel.*

Bohemians met at Les Deux Magots back in the 1920s

ists. The food is anything but light. The restaurant's specialties: pork sausage with remoulade, and stuffed pig's trotters. Extensive menu and rotating daily specials. *Daily | 151, bd. Saint-Germain-des-Prés | 6th arr. | tel. 0145 48 53 91 | M 4 Saint-Germain-des-Prés | www.bras serielipp.fr*

LA COUPOLE ⭐ (152 B3) (*M J10*)

In the 1920s, artists such as Chagall, Picasso and Dalí kept company in this Art Deco temple. The lamb curry is legendary; they've been making it here according to a traditional South Indian recipe since 1927. *Daily | 102, bd. du Montparnasse | 14th arr. | tel. 0143 20 14 20 | M 4 Vavin | www.lacoupole-paris.com*

0147 70 12 06 | M 4, 8, 9 Strasbourg-Saint-Denis | www.julienparis.com

CAFÉS

Paris is famous for its cafés. Here are some of the essential, classic cafés that live up to their historical reputation:

CAFÉ DE FLORE (146 B6) (*M K8*)

An institution and meeting place for artists, literary figures and intellectuals since Simone de Beauvoir, Jean-Paul Sartre and Albert Camus were regulars here. Today, it is a place to see and be seen. *Daily | 172, bd. Saint-Germain | 6th arr. | tel. 0145 48 55 26 | M 4 Saint-Germain-des-Prés | www.cafedeflore.fr*

LES DEUX MAGOTS (146 B6) (*ⓜ K8*)
This famous "café littéraire" — according to its self-promotion — where Ernest Hemingway came to drink whiskey is named after the two Chinese porcelain figures at the entrance. It is a special treat to sit on the terrace facing Saint-Germain-des-Prés church. *Daily | 6, pl. Saint-Germain-des-Prés | 6th arr. | tel. 01 45 48 55 25 | M 4 Saint-Germain-des-Prés | www.lesdeuxmagots.fr*

This is where the 21st-century Parisian literati meet:

LE BARBOUQUIN
(148 C2) (*ⓜ P6*)
Invitingly colourful and unconventional. This 'book bar' is a bookshop, meeting spot for artists, and café all in one, located in the Belleville district, a hot spot for street artists. Regular literary events are held here, as are unannounced theatre performances. *Mon–Fri 9am–7pm, Sat/Sun 10am–8pm | 1, rue Denoyez | 20th arr. | tel. 09 84 32 13 21 | M 2, 11 Belleville | www.facebook.com/lebarbouquin*

If you want to experience today's authentic Paris, the best place to go is any café in a residential district that doesn't attract many tourists. You'll meet real Parisians here, and the coffee will be much cheaper! Drinking your INSIDERTIP coffee at the bar is often less expensive, as well, and you're more likely to fall into conversation with the regulars.

RESTAURANTS: EXPENSIVE

BEL CANTO ★ (147 E5) (*ⓜ M8*)
A unique restaurant in which trained opera singers, accompanied by a piano, belt out arias by Verdi, Puccini and others as you enjoy the fine Italian cuisine. A dining experience based on the motto "les diners lyriques". *Daily (evenings only) | 72, quai de l'Hôtel de Ville | 4th arr. | tel. 01 42 78 30 18 | M 1, 11 Hôtel de Ville | www.lebelcanto.com*

LE BÉLIER ★ (146 C5) (*ⓜ K8*)
This illustrious restaurant evokes the paintings of the Dutch painter Jan Vermeer. Star designer Jacques Garcia has transformed this intimate restaurant in the elegant *L'Hôtel* into a real gem. At lunchtime, you can order a three-course meal from Michelin-starred chef Julien Montbabut starting from 55 euros. In the evenings, there's nothing under five courses, and prices are 110 euros and

MARCO POLO HIGHLIGHTS

up. For the price, you'll be served plates adorned with true works of haute cuisine art. *Daily (Aug closed Sun/Mon) | 13, rue des Beaux Arts | 6th arr. | tel. 01 44 41 99 00 | M 4 Saint-Germain-des-Prés | www.l-hotel.com*

CITRUS ETOILE (144 C1) (𝄚 F5)

Excellent cuisine – classical French dishes with a modern interpretation including Asian and Californian influences – originate from Gilles Epié's kitchen. Com-

fortably discreet atmosphere and only a few yards from the Arc de Triomphe. *Closed Sat/Sun | 6, rue Arsène Houssaye | 8th arr. | tel. 01 42 89 15 51 | M 1, 2, 6, RER A Charles de Gaulle-Etoile | www. citrusetoile.fr*

1728 (146 A2) (𝄚 J6)

If you've ever wanted to try signature wines, this is the place! This restaurant has been pairing fine wines with avant-garde cuisine since – you guessed it – 1728. For

FAVOURITE EATERIES

Marketplace (149 D2–3) (𝄚 P5–6)

Young globetrotter Virginie Godard has shown Parisians that street food can be cheap and delicious: Her *Food Market* is a huge success. It's a culinary trip around the world, including vegetarian dishes, African cuisine, and foods traditional at Chinese New Year. Mothers, hipsters and businessmen alike come together here to enjoy a good meal. *2 Thursdays per month 6pm–10.30pm | blvd de Belleville between métro stations Couronnes and Ménilmontant | 18th arr. | tel. 01 42 28 35 91 | M2 Couronnes or Ménilmontant | www.lefoodmarket.fr*

Leftovers (143 E1) (𝄚 Q1)

Food that defies our throwaway society: *Freegan Pony* uses leftover supermarket products in its dishes, and guests pay whatever they can afford or want to contribute. It's the brainchild of squatter Aladdin Charni. In late 2015, he served one of his "leftover" meals in an illegally occupied building. The idea and the food were so well-received that the city is now providing official support for the initiative. *Reopening after renovations |*

Place Auguste Baron | 19th arr. | M 7 Porte de la Vilette | www.freeganpony.com

Tartines en Seine ⊗ (147 E6) (𝄚 M8)

Jean-Paul Dufour's Street Food Bike is like a food truck, but more environmentally friendly. His bike has a mobile kitchen where he prepares traditional French *tartines* (open-faced sandwiches) – with fresh ingredients on organic bread, naturally. *Depending on the weather Feb–Nov | right Seine bank near Hôtel de Ville | 4th arr. | M 1, 11 Hôtel de Ville | www.facebook.com/tartine senseine*

Bread. Filled (147 F2) (𝄚 M5)

It's small, but it will surprise you: *Urfa Dürüm* makes the city's best Kurdish sandwiches! The pitta bread is prepared right in front of you and filled with fresh ingredients, and you sit on low wooden stools. If that sounds uncomfortable, you can take your food and stroll over to the nearby Canal Saint-Martin. *Daily noon–midnight | 58, rue du Faubourg Saint-Denis | 10th arr. | tel. 01 48 24 12 84 | M 4 Château d'Eau*

the price, you'll experience a journey back in time to the 18th century, when Madame Pompadour was a regular here. *Closed Sat lunchtime, closed Sun | 8, rue d'Anjou | 8th arr. | tel. 01 40 17 04 77 | M 1, 8, 12 Concorde | www.restaurant-1728.com*

LES OMBRES ★ ⚄ (144 C4) (⬚ F7)

You will not find a more spectacular view of the Eiffel Tower than through the glass roof of this restaurant at the Musée du Quai Branly – Jacques Chirac. In the summer you can enjoy the imaginatively prepared meals – variations of French classics – and the exquisite atmosphere from the terrace. *Daily | 27, quai Branly | 7th arr. | tel. 01 47 53 68 00 | M 9 Iéna | www.lesombres-restaurant.com*

LE TRAIN BLEU ★ ●
(154 C2) (⬚ O–P10)

Without a doubt the most exquisite station restaurant in the world. The 20-foot-high ceilings are reminiscent of a dining hall at Versailles. Should you find the prices for the classic French cuisine too prohibitive, opt for a cocktail and enjoy the glorious atmosphere in one of the comfortable leather armchairs in the bar. *Daily | pl. Louis Armand | 12th arr. | tel. 01 43 43 09 06 | M 1, 14, RER A, D Gare de Lyon | www.le-train-bleu.com*

RESTAURANTS: MODERATE

ALCAZAR (146 C6) (⬚ K8)

A freshly renovated hot spot for jetsetters, with a glass roof and lots of greenery. The restaurant is upscale: A paltry 72 euros will buy you 30 g of caviar as a starter. The bar upstairs also offers snacks big and small – so the cocktails won't knock you out! DJ on Wed–Sat from 10 pm. *Daily (Aug closed Sun/Mon) | 62, rue Mazarine | 6th arr. | tel. 01 53 10 19 99 | M 4, 10 Odéon | www.alcazar.fr*

After-dinner coffee: Style and tradition at 1728, since 1728

BOUILLON RACINE (153 D1) (⬚ L9)

Gorgeous Art Nouveau ornamentation winds around two storeys of windows, mirrors and wood panelling in a pleasing shade of green. Even the mosaic floor has been meticulously restored in this former workers' cafeteria. The traditional French cuisine includes snails, foie gras or pot-au-feu. *Daily | 3, rue Racine | 6th arr. | tel. 01 44 32 15 60 | M 10 , RER B Cluny-La Sorbonne | www.bouillon-racine. com*

CAFÉ MARLY ● ⚄ (146 C4) (⬚ K7)

Chic restaurant at the Louvre with a stellar view of the pyramid. Naturally, at this café, you're not just paying for the modern French cuisine – the main attraction is the location. The international guests you'll encounter here are either well-heeled or just enjoying a special treat. *Daily | Palais du Louvre | 93, rue de Rivoli | 1st arr. | tel. 01 49 26 06 60 | M 1, 7 Palais Royal-Musée du Louvre | www.cafe-marly.com*

INSIDER TIP CALIFE (146 C5) *(ⅲ K8)*
"Paris, the city of love". Some clichés exist for a reason, and this two-hour cruise (9–11pm) along the islands of the Seine might be one of those reasons! With a three-course menu (from 67 euros including boat ticket), the organisers hope to prove that Paris has earned its moniker. Make sure to reserve tickets early! *Daily | Quai Malaquais | near the Pont des Arts | 6th arr. | tel. 01 43 54 50 04 | M 1 Louvre-Rivoli | www.calife.com*

L'ESCARGOT MONTORGUEIL ★
(147 E4) *(ⅲ L7)*
A traditional restaurant established in 1832, decorated in the Empire style. Luminaries such as Marcel Proust, Charlie Chaplin, Pablo Picasso and Jacqueline Kennedy have dined here. The name *escargot* – snail – says it all. You can sample numerous different variations on these molluscs here. Snails with parsley and garlic butter are especially popular, whilst snails with foie gras or black truffles are a posh treat. You can even try exotic curry snails! But don't worry: You don't *have* to eat snails here. The upscale menu has something for everyone – even vegetarians. *Daily | 38, rue Montorgueil | 1st arr. | tel. 01 42 36 83 51 | M 4 Etienne Marcel | www.escargotmontorgueil.com*

AU VIEUX PARIS (147 E6) *(ⅲ M8)*
Located next to Notre-Dame, this is where the canons lived back in 1512. Today, the owners Odette and Georges de Larochebrochard cordially welcome their guests. Traditional French cuisine has been served here since 1750! The exuberantly plush furnishings with a Gothic touch create a romantic atmosphere; the set meal is substantial and not expensive by Parisian standards. *Daily | 24, rue Chanoinesse | 4th arr. | tel. 01 40 51 78 52 | M 4 Cité | www.restaurantauvieuxparis.fr*

MACEO (146 C3) *(ⅲ L6)*
Innovative, contemporary restaurant with a large, light and comfortable dining area. Also serves vegetarian dishes. A small library and bar entice you to lin-

Au Vieux Paris: blossoming purple wisteria adorns the entrance and courtyard

ger a little longer. *Closed Sat for lunch and Sun | 15, rue des Petits-Champs | 1st arr. | tel. 01 42 97 53 85 | M 3 Bourse | www.maceorestaurant.com*

LE P'TIT TROQUET
(145 D5) *(𝑚 G8)*

Tiny bistro with an authentic 1920s flair, cordially serving sophisticated and refined traditional French cuisine such as "homemade foie gras with fig chutney". A good value for money, especially considering its close proximity to the Eiffel Tower. *Closed Sat lunch and Sun/Mon | 28, rue de l'Exposition | 7th arr. | tel. 01 85 15 24 64 | M8 Ecole Militaire | www.leptittroquet.fr*

INSIDER TIP SOYA ⊛
(148 B3) *(𝑚 O6)*

Vegetarian/vegan restaurant near the Canal Saint-Martin. 100 per cent organic. Light, airy space with parquet floors, wooden tables and an open kitchen. Christel Dhuit and her team now serve fusion food in this former plumbers' workshop. On the weekends, hip Parisians come here for a hearty, healthy brunch after a night of drinking and partying. *Closed Mon, Tue lunchtime, Sun evenings | 20, Rue de la Pierre Levée | 11th arr. | tel. 01 85 15 28 02 | M 11 Goncourt | www.soya-cantine-bio.fr*

LE SUD
(138 A6) *(𝑚 E4)*

Guests have the feeling of being in a village in the South of France under a vaulted glass roof. Pleasant atmosphere, friendly service and tasty Provençal specialities. A reservation is necessary at this much-loved restaurant. *Daily | 91, bd. Gouvion Saint Cyr | 17th arr. | tel. 01 45 74 02 77 | M 1 Porte Maillot | RER C Neuilly – Porte Maillot | www.le-sud-restaurant.com*

RESTAURANTS: BUDGET

BISTROT RICHELIEU (146 C3) *(𝑚 K7)*

The comfortable atmosphere in this restaurant is exactly what you need after an exhausting visit to the neighbouring Louvre. Typical French dishes such as snails, onion soup and duck grace the tables. *Closed Sun and Aug | 45, rue de Richelieu | 1st arr. | tel. 01 42 60 19 16 | M 1, 7 Palais Royal | www.bistrotrichelieu.com*

INSIDER TIP CAFÉ A (147 F1) *(𝑚 N5)*

Only insiders are aware of the hip meeting spot for artists – including a café, bar and restaurant – behind the walls of this former monastery next to the Gare de l'Est. It offers international cuisine, from Italian and Lebanese to Japanese. Wide selection of ⊛ organic wines. Particularly recommendable in good weather – then you can eat under the trees of the monastery garden. *Sun/Mon 10am–5pm, Tue–Sat 10am–2am | 148, rue du Faubourg Saint-Martin | 10th arr. | tel. 07 71 61 10 38 | M 4, 5, 7 Gare de l'Est | www.cafea.fr*

CHANTAIRELLE (153 E2) *(𝑚 M10)*

This restaurant pays homage to the Auvergne region. Except for the ice cream, everything on the menu comes from that part of central France. The rich, flavourful cuisine is a perfect fit for the rustic ambience and the charming little courtyard. If you enjoy the food, you can also purchase Auvergnese delicacies to take home with you, such as sausages, cheese or lentils. *Mon–Sat (Mon lunch only, Sat evening only) | 17, rue Laplace | 5th arr. | tel. 01 46 33 18 59 | M 10 Cardinal Lemoine | www.chantairelle.com*

CHEZ GLANDINES (153 E6) *(𝑚 M12)*

This restaurant on the Butte aux Cailles is where young, hungry Parisians go to eat hearty southwestern French meals on the cheap. And the restaurant doesn't take reservations: Waiting outside with a glass of wine and good company is part of the experience. *Daily | 30, rue des cinq Diamants | 13th arr. | tel. 01 45 80 70 10 | M 6 Corvisart | www.chezgladines-but teauxcailles.fr*

CHEZ MARIANNE (147 F5) *(m N8)*
This busy restaurant with a terrace and a delicatessen is located around the corner from the lively rue des Rosiers at the centre of the Marais district. Try the popular Middle Eastern appetiser plat-

ter. *Daily | 2, rue des Hospitalières Saint-Gervais | 4th arr. | tel. 01 42 72 18 86 | M 1 Saint-Paul*

HOPE CAFÉ ⚛ (141 D3) *(m L3)*
Located behind Sacré-Cœur, this modern restaurant with its own food shop specializes in organic foods. It goes without saying that there are plenty of vegetarian options. The smoothies to take away are particularly popular. *Closed Mon | 64, rue Lamarck | 18th arr. | tel. 01 46 06 54 40 | M 12 Lamarck-Caulaincourt | www.hope-cafe.com*

INSIDER TIP ▶ LA FOURMI AILÉE (153 E1) *(m M9)*
The atmosphere in the "winged ant", not far from Notre-Dame, is relaxed and cosy. The loaded bookshelves lining the walls bear witness to a time when books were still sold here. Today, you can dine on quiches, salads, traditional meat dishes, and even vegetarian meals in this historic location. It's also the perfect place to stop for a cup of tea or espresso while you're on the go. *Daily | 8, rue du Fouarre | 5th arr. | tel. 01 43 29 40 99 | | M 10 Cluny-La Sorbonne | www.parisresto.com*

LE MESTURET (146 C2) *(m L6)*
This locale has maintained its high standards of quality since it won the award for Bistro of the Year in 2012. In the mood for a veal stew just like grandma would make, a classic steak tartare or potatoes au gratin? Then this is the place for you! *Daily | 77, rue de Richelieu | 2nd arr. | tel. 01 42 97 40 68 | M 3 Bourse | www.lemes turet.com*

LES PAPILLES (153 D3) *(m L10)*
The name of the "back from the market" menu, which changes every day, speaks for itself. If you enjoy your meal, you can pop into the deli afterwards and load

LOW BUDGET

Strapped for cash? No worries! On their website, Thomas and Romain tell you which restaurants in Paris serve meals for about 10 euros. The two men test the quality of all the restaurants personally. They only list restaurants that serve homemade dishes with fresh, local ingredients. *www.lespetitestables.com*

You'll find the city's most affordable coffee at the non-profit *Café des Petits Frères* **(139 F4)** *(m H3) (Mon–Sat 9am–12.30pm, Mon, Wed–Fri also 2pm–6pm | 47, rue des Batignolles | 17th arr. | tel. 01 42 93 84 41 | www. petitsfreresdespauvres.fr/nos-implantations/75017-02---le-cafe-des-petits-freres-des-pauvres.html | M 2 Rome)*. It's a project to help prevent senior citizens from becoming socially isolated. The full breakfast for €1.60 is served by volunteers from *petits frères des pauvres*. It's the perfect way to meet locals.

up your bags with goodies. *Closed Sun/ Mon | 30, rue Gay Lussac | 5th arr. | tel. 01 43 25 20 79 | RER B Luxembourg | www.lespapillesparis.fr*

LA RECYCLERIE  (141 D1) *(m L1)*

Hip vintage-style café/restaurant with an urban farm and repair workshop in a former train station near the Saint-Ouen

Peruse – discuss – sample: the selection is impossibly irresistible at Chez Marianne

PAUSE CAFÉ 148 C6) *(m P9)*

The "coffee break" is a cool restaurant in a cool quarter right behind the bastille. Whether for a meal or just a cup of coffee or a glass on the terrace: if you like it young and stylish, then this is the address for you. Uncomplicated bistrot cuisine. *Daily (Sun only until 8pm) | 41, rue de Charonne | 11th arr. | tel. 01 48 06 80 33 | M 1, 5, 8 Bastille*

À LA POMPONNETTE (140 C4) *(m K3)*

Time seems to have stood still here at the foot of Montmartre. This bar and restaurant serves generous helpings of hearty French food. *Daily | 42, rue Lepic | 18th arr. | tel. 01 46 06 08 36 | M 2 Blanche | www.pomponnette-montmartre.com*

flea market. The eatery serves sustainable cuisine with fresh ingredients and minimal meat. Kitchen waste is fed directly to the chickens (yes, you can even find chickens in Paris!) or used as compost for the vegetable garden along the disused railway tracks. In good weather, you can sit outdoors. It's a little oasis of green, shielded from the bustle of the big city. *Mon–Thu noon–midnight, Fri/Sat noon–2am, Sun 11am–10pm | 83, blvd. Ornano | 18th arr. | tel. 01 42 57 58 49 | M 4 Porte de Clignancourt | www.larecyclerie.com*

SATURNE  (147 D2) *(m L6)*

Trendy restaurant with austere wooden furnishings under a glass roof and

LOCAL SPECIALITIES

bœuf bourguignon – braised beef in a Burgundy sauce

bouillabaisse – fish stew made with Mediterranean fish

brochettes de coquilles Saint Jacques – kebabs with scallops

caneton à l'orange – roast duck in an orange sauce (photo right)

coq au vin – braise of chicken in red wine, but sometimes in Riesling

côtes de porc aux herbes – pork chops with herbs

crème brûlée – a rich custard base topped with a layer of hard caramel

crêpes Suzette – thin pancakes with Grand Marnier

écrevisses à la nage – boiled crayfish in a spicy broth

escargots à la bourguignonne – boiled Burgundy snails served in their shells

fruits de mer – seafood, e.g. *crevettes* (prawns, photo left) or *huîtres* (oysters) – often served raw

gigot d'agneau aux morilles – leg of lamb with morels

gratin dauphinois – potato gratin

homard à l'armoricaine – lobster in a tomato, garlic, herb, white wine and cognac sauce

moules marinières – mussels steamed in white wine with onions

noisettes d'agneau – small lamb cutlets fried in butter

pot-au-feu – stew with beef, chicken and a variety of vegetables

profiteroles – small cream puff-pastry with vanilla ice cream and chocolate sauce

quenelles de brochet – pickerel, cream and egg dumplings

ratatouille – vegetables sauteed with olive oil, onions and herbs, served either hot or cold

soupe à l'oignon gratinée – onion soup baked with cheese

tarte Tatin – carmelised upside down apple tart

an excellent vinotheque in the lobby. The fresh, uncomplicated, mostly organic cuisine places great value on the freshness of the products used –outstanding! *Closed Sat/Sun | 17, rue* *Notre-Dame-des-Victoires | 2nd arr. | tel. 0142603190 | M3 Bourse | www. saturne-paris.fr*

INSIDERTIP **LE VIEUX BELLEVILLE** ●
(149 E2) (*Q5*)

Alongside hearty French food, you can enjoy singalongs of French chansons. Don't know the lyrics? No problem! They hand out lyric sheets, and then it begins: "Padam, padam, padam..." On Tuesdays, Edith Piaf is on the programme. The brainchild of Joseph Pantaleo aka "Jojo", who was born a few houses down the road over half a century ago, is a popular place, so it's best to make reservations. *Closed Sun | live music to sing along to Tue, Thu–Sat 8pm–2am | 12, Rue des Envierges | 20th arr. | tel. 01 44 62 92 66 | M 11 Pyrénées | www.le-vieux-belleville.com*

WINE BARS

INSIDERTIP **LE BARON ROUGE**
(154 C1) (*P9*)

A small wine bar with a special flair. It is particularly lively in the Baron Rouge, on Sunday at lunch when, after shopping at the nearby Marché d'Aligre, the Parisians stand together around wine barrels in front of the bar enjoying a glass of wine and oysters. *Daily | 1, rue Théophile-Roussel | 12th arr. | tel. 01 43 43 14 32 | M 8 Ledru-Rollin | www.lebaronrouge.net*

LE COUDE FOU (147 F5) (*N8*)

A typical wine bar, sadly rare in Paris. Large selection, simple wooden tables and bistro cuisine from a small menu. *Daily | 12, rue du Bourg-Tibourg | 4th arr. | tel. 01 42 77 15 16 | M 1, 11 Hôtel de Ville | www.lecoudefou.fr*

LE RUBIS (146 B3) (*K6*)

The simple wine bar has remained virtually unchanged since its opening in 1948. Large wine selection, cheese platter and always a traditional daily special. *Closed Sun | 10, rue du Marché Saint-Honoré | 1st arr. | tel. 01 42 61 03 34 | M 8, 14 Pyramides | www.facebook.com/Le-Rubis-964093417031887*

Le Rubis: chatting over a glass of red wine with friends and neighbours

SHOPPING

WHERE TO START?

CITY

If you're not looking for cheap clothing or practically unwearable haute couture and want to avoid the stress of department store clutter, you're best off in **Marais (148 A–B 3–6)** *(⌞ M–O 6–8)*. You'll find plenty of shops where French women buy their working day wardrobe. Men can also find what they're looking for. Select hand-crafted items and cosmetics round off your shopping spree and a break at one of the street cafés in the district always turns shopping into a pleasurable event.

Shopping in the French consumer metropolis conjures up images of fashion, perfumes, delicatessens, champagne and other luxury items. In Paris, everything is done to the hilt and products are always showcased with élan.

A shopping spree in Paris means digging deeper into your pockets than at home. Paris offers the best of everything and, if you know where to shop, you can even land a good bargain. Apart from that, wandering through the shrines to consumerism and shopping streets, *lèche vitrines* (window shopping), as they say in French, has sheer entertainment value. Whether it's the haute couture shop windows or a grocery store's lavish and colourful displays: shopping in Paris is an

Très chic, très riche: – you can find everything in Paris. In this glittering metropolis, the only limits are set by your wallet

experience. Some even make a special trip to take advantage of clearance sales *(soldes)* that occur twice a year (Jan and June/July).

Most shops are open Monday–Saturday from 10am to 7.30pm. On Thursdays large department stores have longer opening hours known as *nocturne,* evening shopping, and close at either 9pm or 10pm. If you want to shop on Sunday, stores in Marais, the lower ground floor at the Louvre and some shops on the Champs-Elysées are open. Many of the small grocers *(épiceries)* never seem to close: in France there is no law regulating closing time for shops. Note, however, that some of the smaller stores close on Monday, Wednesday, or over lunchtime. Department stores and many other shops are open on the last three or four Sundays before Christmas. Opening hours are only listed in this section if they differ from these general rules.

First-class caviar is only one of the specialities to be found at Fauchon

ANTIQUES

DROUOT (146 C1) (*Ø L5*)

As one of the oldest auction houses in the world, Drouot is an institution. Furniture and art objects come under the hammer in 16 halls. Like a visit to a museum! *9, rue Drouot | 9th arr. | M 8, 9 Richelieu-Drouot | www.drouot.com*

INSIDER TIP VILLAGE SAINT-PAUL (148 A6) (*Ø N8*)

90 different shops are situated in several interconnected, idyllic back courtyards near the Place des Vosges where you'll find small pieces of furniture, paintings, jewellery, porcelain and more. *Wed–Mon | between rue Saint-Paul and rue Charlemagne | 4th arr. | M 1 Saint-Paul | www.levillagesaintpaul.com*

VINTAGE PHOTOGRAPHIE (148 A4) (*Ø N7*)

The digital age seems to have passed this shop by. Photographer Fabien Breuvart sells artefacts from the previous century; the snapshots cost between 7 and 130 euros and are sorted by size and carefully wrapped in transparent foil. The wall next to the front door of the shop serves as an exhibition space for a range of different photo projects. *35–37, rue Charlot | 3th arr. | M 8 Filles du Calvaire | www.imagesetportraits.fr*

BOOKS & MUSIC

LES BOUQUINISTES (146–147 B–E 4–6) (*Ø K–M 7–8*)

The green wooden boxes on both sides of the Seine have shaped the cityscape for more than 300 years. It's a real kick to rummage through the old books, newspapers and postcards. *Between Jardin des Tuileries and the Île Saint-Louis | 1st arr./5th arr. | M 7 Pont Neuf*

FNAC ● (145 D2) (*Ø G6*)

The largest bookseller in Paris also has a large CD and DVD department. An excellent place to while away a few hours on a rainy day. *Mon–Sat until 10.30pm,*

Sun until 8.45pm | 74, av. des Champs-Elysées | 8th arr. | M 1, 9 Franklin D. Roosevelt | www.fnac.com

DELICATESSEN

BARTHÉLEMY ⭐ (146 A6) (*J8*)

One of the best cheese emporiums (*crèmeries*) in Paris, it also caters to Élysée Palace. Former President Charles de Gaulle once remarked: "How can anyone govern a nation that has more kinds of cheese than days of the year?" The aromas of many of these cheeses waft through this small shop. 51, rue de Grenelle | 7th arr. | M 12 Rue du Bac

DEBAUVE & GALLAIS ⭐
(146 B5) (*K8*)

The opulent, 200-year-old chocolaterie can be compared to a jewellery shop. The big difference: these gems melt in your mouth. 30, rue des Saint-Pères | 7th arr. | M 4 Saint-Germain-des-Prés | www.debauve-et-gallais.com

FAUCHON (146 A2) (*J6*)

Gourmands and ordinary consumers alike can appreciate the celestial selection of exotic fruits, truffles and caviar in this gourmet shop. 26, pl. de la Madeleine | 8th arr. | M 8, 12, 14 Madeleine | www.fauchon.fr

HÉDIARD (146 A2) (*J6*)

This long standing delicatessen (founded in 1854) is known for its variety of treats in exquisitely packed little tins, especially the truffled foie gras and lobster pâté, which make appropriate souvenirs. 21, pl. de la Madeleine | 8th arr. | M 8, 12, 14 Madeleine | www.hediard.fr

INSIDER TIP IZRAËL (147 F5) (*N8*)

Specialities from all over the world, mainly Arabian, African and Asian countries, are piled to the rafters in wild confusion amid the sausages hanging from hooks and the exotic spices. A unique aromatic experience. 30, rue François Miron | 4th arr. | M 1 Saint-Paul

LADURÉE (146 A3) (*J6*)

The king of macarons. Apart from traditional flavours like chocolate, vanilla, coffee, orange blossom or rose, you'll also find seasonal varieties here, like violet or cinnamon. Also worth a visit: The magnificent 19th-century *salon de thé* with its opulent ceiling frescoes. Mon–Sat 8am–8pm, Sun 9am–7pm | 16–18, Rue Royale | 8th arr. | M 8, 12, 14 Madeleine | www.laduree.fr

⭐ **Barthélemy**
A paradise for cheese lovers within a tiny space → p. 75

⭐ **Debauve & Gallais**
A chocolaterie which resembles an upscale jewellery store → p. 75

⭐ **Marché aux Puces**
Probably the world's largest flea market, in Saint-Ouen → p. 77

⭐ **Le Bon Marché**
The most elegant department store in all of Paris → p. 78

⭐ **Rue du Faubourg Saint-Honoré**
The haute couture area of the city → p. 79

⭐ **Place des Victoires**
Young fashion designers and lots of boutiques → p. 79

MARCO POLO HIGHLIGHTS

LAVINIA (146 B2) (*ᗯ J6*)

The ultimate wine shop. 6,500 wines from more than 30 countries on three floors, at prices ranging from under 10 euros to bottles costing several thousand. ◑ Large selection of organic wines. You can test the wine (without a surcharge) together with a snack in the accompanying bar. *3, bd. de la Madeleine | 1st arr. | M 8, 12, 14 Madeleine | www.lavinia.fr*

LEGRAND FILLES & FILS (146 C3) (*ᗯ L6*)

A mouth-watering delicatessen shop situated between the nostalgic Galleries Vivienne and rue de la Banque. The shop was established in 1880 and exudes time-honoured elegance. Wine connoisseurs in particular will clamour to experience the extensive wine selection and wine tastings at the bar's wooden counters. *1, rue de la Banque | 2nd arr. | M 1, 7 Palais-Royal | www.caves-legrand.com*

INSIDER TIP MAISON STOHRER (147 D3) (*ᗯ L6*)

What a dream! This shop is like a blast from the past. The oldest confectionary in Paris was established in 1730 by the court pastry chef of Louis XV. Even today, delicacies such as the *baba au rhum* are made according to the old recipes. *51, rue Montorgueil | 2nd arr. | M 3 Sentier | www.stohrer.fr*

MAISON DE THÉ GEORGE CANNON ● ◑ (152 B2) (*ᗯ J10*)

You can choose from over 250 types of tea. The venerable establishment is much more than a tea shop. In addition to tastings in the bar, light organic dishes are served in the salon. Shiatsu massages or an authentic Japanese tea ceremony on the shop's lower level are a good way to unwind. *12, Notre-Dame-des Champs | 6th arr. | M 4 St.-Placide | www.georgecannon.fr*

MARIAGE FRÈRES (138 C6) (*ᗯ F5*)

The original source for top-quality tea blends from this internationally renowned, traditional Parisian brand. You can sample a steaming brew in the adjoining tea salon, decorated in elegant colonial style. The little INSIDER TIP *tea museum* on the first floor bears witness to the company's long history. *30, rue du Bourg-Tibourg | 4th arr. | M 1, 11 Hôtel de Ville | www.mariagefreres.com*

LA PÂTISSERIE DES RÊVES (146 A6) (*ᗯ J9*)

Tartes au citron, mille-feuilles, éclaires ... decadent indulgences of French confectionary art await under bell jars and entice you to buy and savour. Tue–Sat 9am–8pm, Sun 9am–6pm | 93, rue du Bac | 7th arr. | M 12 Rue du Bac | www.lapatisseriedesreves.com

ROSE BAKERY ◑ (148 C6) (*ᗯ L4*)

The absolute "in" place among young and dynamic Parisian "bobos" who love to enjoy English-style baked goods or the imaginative vegetarian snacks made with organic ingredients in minimalist surroundings. *46, rue des Martyrs | 9th arr. | M 12 Saint-Georges | www.rosebakery.fr*

DESIGN & LIFESTYLE

ARTY DANDY (146 B6) (*ᗯ K8*)

A shop for those who have everything. It sees itself as a gallery-store, and anything in terms of art, kitsch, fashion, cosmetics and design as well as the extraordinary, including individual pieces and limited editions, can be bought here. *1, rue de Furstemberg | 6th arr. |*

M 4 St.-Germain-des-Prés | www.arty dandy.com

DEHILLERIN
(147 D4) *(ⓜ L7)*

In this shop, steeped in tradition since 1820, you will find everything that has to do with kitchens and cooking on its two floors. Dehillerin is world-renowned among chefs and French celebrity chefs also frequent this shop. *18 and 20, rue Coquillière | 1st arr. | M/RER Châtelet-Les Halles | www.e-dehillerin.fr*

MARCHÉ SAINT PIERRE
(149 D4) *(ⓜ L3)*

Covering five floors and over 26,900 square feet, this somewhat older department store stocks rolls of fabric at unbeatable prices. Many women from the nearby African neighbourhood scour the shelves for the right materials. Rows of fabric shops line the whole area in this paradise for those who sew. *2, rue Charles Nodier | 18th arr. | M2 Anvers | www.marchesaintpierre.com*

FLEA MARKETS

ALIGRE (154 C1) *(ⓜ P9)*

The very beautiful Marché d'Aligre is the oldest flea market in Paris. The prices are quite affordable and even groceries can be purchased here. *Tue–Sun mornings | 1e, pl. d'Aligre | 12th arr. | M 8 Ledru-Rollin*

SAINT-OUEN ★
(140–141 C--E1) *(ⓜ K--L1)*

With more than 3,000 stalls, the *Marché aux Puces de Saint-Ouen* is the world's largest flea market. You can purchase almost everything here. The grounds at the Porte de Clignancourt encompass a range of 15 markets. To see them all you'll have to cover around 10 miles. For a bit of refreshment along the way, we recommend the rustic tav-

The whole *marché aux puces* in Saint-Ouen is as colourful as these pictures

ern *Chez Louisette (130, av. Michelet)* with live music on the *Marché Vernaison*. *Sat 9am–6pm, Sun 10am–6pm, Mon 11am–5pm | 18th arr. | M 4 Porte de Clignancourt | www.marcheauxpuces-saintouen.com*

VANVES (151 D6) (*𝄞 0*)

The Marché aux Puces de la Porte de Vanves, covering no more than two streets, is the smallest flea market in Paris. On one street, you'll find a mix of new and old clothes, shoes and handbags, while the other one is a haven for novelties and furniture of all kinds. *Sat/Sun 7am–2pm | av. Georges Lafenestre*

Trendy shoes by Monderer can be found on rue des Francs-Bourgeois

and av. Marc Sangnier | 14th arr. | M 13 Porte de Vanves | www.pucesdevanves.fr

DEPARTMENT STORES

LE BON MARCHÉ ⭐ (152 A1) (*𝄞 J9*)

The oldest department store in Paris and a symbol of luxury and quality for over 150 years. It is still a joy to meander through this Belle-Époque gem with unobtrusive classical music in the background, away from the usual touristy hustle and bustle. One of the best shoe and fashion departments in town. The *gourmet food section (www.lagrandeepicerie.fr)* next to it is quite an experience! *24, rue de Sèvres | 7th arr. | M 10, 12 Sèvres Babylone | www.lebonmarche.com*

GALERIES LAFAYETTE (146 B1) (*𝄞 K5*)

The shrine to consumerism situated under a massive glass dome has been a huge attraction since 1908. Clothing is arranged by brand name, as opposed to the type of garment (trousers, shirts, etc.) The shoe department is the largest in the world covering nearly 10,000 square feet. If you need a break from shopping, there's a variety of restaurants and a free 🍃 roof terrace with a panoramic view. *40, bd. Haussmann | 9th arr. | M 3, 7, 8 Opéra | RER A Auber | www.galerieslafayette.com.* The opening of a branch on the Champs-Elysées (no. 52) is planned for 2018.

LE PRINTEMPS (146 C1) (*𝄞 K5*)

In addition to the huge cosmetics department on the ground floor and the beautiful spa area on the first floor, the upper floor is devoted to all the luxury fashion brands as well as less costly labels beyond the café-restaurant under the famous Art Nouveau glass dome. *64, bd. Haussmann | 9th arr. | M 3, 9 Havre-Caumartin | RER A Auber | www.printemps.com*

CLOTHING & ACCESSORIES

On *Avenue Montaigne* **(145 D3)**(*ω G6*) and ★ ● *rue du Faubourg Saint-Honoré* **(146 A–B3)**(*ω H–K 5–6*) you'll find all the well-known names in fashion: Armani, Chanel, Dior, Gucci, Hermès, Lacroix, Max Mara, Versace, etc. Younger and bolder fashion labels are located around the ★ *Place des Victoires* **(147 D3)** (*ω L6*) while in Marais, especially in and around *rue des Francs-Bourgeois* **(148 A–B5)** (*ω N–O8*) more unconventional fashion boutiques such as Abu d'abi, Azzedine Alaia, Issey Miyake and Paule Ka have opened up.

The term *prêt-à-porter* means wearable garments that are partly influenced by haute couture. Bargain hunters will be interested in the *degriffé* offers: reduced brand name clothing from the previous season from which most of the company labels have been removed. A group of shops that also offer outlet items is located on the INSIDERTIP▶ *rue d'Alésia* **(152 A6)** (*ω J12*), e.g. Sonja By (no. 110) or Cacharel (no. 114). Some labels are marked down by 40 percent or even more during clearance sales.

The Christian Lacroix boutique on rue du Faubourg Saint-Honoré

BIJOUX MONIC **(148 A4–5)** (*ω N8*)
The small jewellery store in one of the most lively shopping streets in the Marais district prides itself on its assortment of more than 10,000 pieces of jewellery with prices between 1 and 10,000 euros. Check it out! *Mon–Sat 10am–7pm, Sun noon–7pm | 14, rue de l'ancienne Comédie | 6th arr. | M 4, 10 Odéon | www. bijouxmonic.com*

CHRISTIAN LOUBOUTIN
(155 D4) (*ω L7*)
The dizzying high heels designed by Christian Louboutin with equally dizzying price tags look their best in the window of the designer's first Parisian boutique. *19, rue Jean-Jaques Rousseau | Galerie Véro Dodat | 1st arr. | M 1 Louvre-Rivoli | www.christianlouboutin.com*

COLETTE **(146 B3)** (*ω K7*)
Fashion, design and everything that's ultra trendy. If you're looking for something out of the ordinary, you've come to the right place. But the prices are also exceptional – exceptionally high. *213, rue Saint-Honoré | 1st arr. | M 1 Tuileries | www.colette.fr*

DÉPÔT VENTE DE PASSY
(144 A5) (*ω D8*)
The Dépôt sells luxury brands at outlet prices and good bargains are guaranteed. *14, rue de la Tour | 16th arr. | M 6 Trocadéro | www.depot-vente-luxe.fr*

INSIDER TIP▶ L'ECLAIREUR
(147 F5) (*m N8*)

The shop has an interesting concept with a mix of object design and names such as Issey Miyake, Prada, Helmut Lange, Comme des Garçons. *26, av. des Champs-Elysées | 8th arr. | M , 9 Franklin D. Roosevelt | www.leclaireur.com*

GERARD DAREL (148 A5) (*m N8*)
One of the major affordable French fashion labels for women's clothing. The trousers, dresses and jackets exude a sporty elegance. *41, rue des Francs-Bourgeois | 4th arr. | M 1 Saint Paul | www.gerarddarel. com*

LOW BUDGET

Second-hand: designer clothing in excellent condition but requiring a bit of rummaging – can be found at *Chercheminippes* **(152 A2)** (*m J9*). *(102, 106, 109, 110, 111, 114, 124 rue du Cherche-Midi | 6th arr. | M 10 Vaneau | www.chercheminippes.com).*

At *Emmaüs* **(148 C6)** (*m P9*) *(Mon–Sat 11am–7.30pm | 54, rue de Charonne | 11th arr. | M 8 Ledru-Rollin |www.emmaus-alternatives.org)*, the social institution founded by Abbé Pierre, there are bargains galore among second-hand clothing, books, crockery and furniture.

Clearance sales *(soldes)*, which go on for six weeks from the middle of January and from the end of June, are when big-name brands are sold at bargain prices with up to 70 percent off.

FRAGONARD (146 B2) (*m K5*)
The INSIDER TIP▶ *Musée du Parfum (free admission)* of the traditional perfume label Fragonard from Grasse in the South of France is situated in an opulent Napoleon III-style palais near the Opéra Garnier. The aim of this operation is, of course, getting you to buy perfume in the showroom at the end of your visit. *Mon–Sat 9am–6pm | 3–5, sq. Louis Jouvet | 9th arr. | M 3, 7, 8 Opéra | www. fragonard.com*

SÉPHORA (145 D2) (*m G6*)
Giant cosmetic and perfume emporium where makeup is applied nonstop as hot disco rhythms play in the background– for free. The chain store's own brand of bath and body products are colourful and pretty. *Mon–Thu 10am–midnight, Fri/Sat 10am–1am | 70–72, av. des Champs-Elysées | 8th arr. | M 1, 2, 6, RER A Charles de Gaulle-Etoile | www.sephora.fr*

ART GALLERIES

The largest assortment of galleries for contemporary art is in the vicinity of the art academy on the *rue de Seine* and its side streets, namely, *rue des Beaux Arts, rue Jacques Callot* and *rue Mazarine* (146 C6) (*m K–L8*).
A similar cluster of galleries is found on *rue Vieille du Temple* (148 A4–5) (*m N7–8*), especially around the Musée Picasso, and on *rue Quincampoix* (147 E4) (*m M7*) by the Centre Georges Pompidou.

INSIDER TIP▶ ART GÉNÉRATION
(147 E5) (*m M8*)
Paris is known as the city of art. Why not acquire an original as a souvenir? In the vicinity of the Centre Pompidou

The shops of the cosmetics chain Sephora are bright and eye-catching

you can choose from paintings, photographs and graphic art from 25 euros upwards! *Tue–Sat 11am–7.30pm, Sun/ Mon 2pm–7.30pm | 67, rue de la Verrerie | 4th arr. | M 1, 11 Hôtel de Ville | www.artgeneration.fr*

VIADUC DES ARTS
(154–155 C–D 2–3) ( O–P 9–10)
Artists and craftsmen have set up studios beneath the viaduct's 60 brick arches. Equally inspiring cafés and restaurants offer refreshment among the approx. 130 shops. *1–129, av. Daumesnil | 12th arr. | M 1, 5, 8 Bastille | www.leviaducdesarts.com*

MARKETS

Nearly every district in Paris has its "own" market, including some ☺ *marchés biologiques* – organic markets. For example, *Marché biologique des Batignolles* (140 A5) (M J3–4) (Sat 9am–2pm | rue des Batignolles | 8th arr./17th arr. | M 2 Rome and M 2, 13

Place de Clichy) or *Marché biologique Brancusi* (152 B3) (M K10) (Sat 9am– 2pm | pl. Constantin Brancusi | 14th arr. | M 13 Gaîté)

MARCHÉ BARBÈS ● (141 E4) (M M3)
Eclectic Arabian-African bazaar, often very chaotic on account of the low prices. *Wed and Sat mornings | bd. de la Chapelle | 18th arr. | M 2, 4 Barbès-Rochechouart*

MARCHÉ DES ENFANTS ROUGES
(148 A4) (M N7)
Paris's oldest food market is inconspicuous. Small, colourful and lively, it's hidden behind houses at the upper end of Le Marais. You'll find more than just stands selling groceries here; there are also lots of little restaurants and street food stalls. The Moroccan food stand INSIDER TIP *Couscous* is highly recommendable; there are often long queues out front. *Tue/Wed, Fri/Sat 8.30am–8.30pm, Thu 8.30am–9.30pm, Sun 8.30am–5pm | 3rd. arr. | M 8 Filles du Calvaire*

ENTERTAINMENT

CITY **WHERE TO START?**
Nightlife in the Bastille quarter can get wild and crazy, particularly on **Rue de Lappe** and **Rue de la Roquette (148 B–C6)** *(🕮 O8–9).* Farther north, along the **Canal Saint-Martin (148 A–B 1–2)** *(🕮 N–O 5–6)* and the **Canal de l'Ourcq (143 D3)** *(🕮 P2–3),* people spread out picnic blankets as soon as the weather permits. Multicultural **Belleville (148–149 C–D 1–2)** *(🕮 P–Q 5–6)* is in the same area. The nightlife on the left bank of the Seine, in the **Saint-Germain-des-Prés (146 B–C 5–6)** *(🕮 J–K 8–9)* quarter, is somewhat more subdued.

Parisian nightlife is legendary and thousands of tourists and Parisians alike are out to catch a glimpse of that unique Parisian flair every night.

Whatever is currently considered trendy changes very quickly in Paris. As soon as a district has been discovered by tourists, the Parisian night scene moves elsewhere. The tendency is to migrate further east, where a pub scene has put down roots in the area around the still-affordable artists' flats. Another district that has been *branché* (hip) for some time is Butte-aux-Cailles near the Place d'Italie with its large number of pubs and relatively reasonable prices.

Pleasure-seekers should be aware that public transport does not operate all night (see p. 127). After 2am, you'll get

Bonne soirée: Paris by night has it all – from extremely expensive to free, from ultra-hip to vintage dives

to your bed by night buses, taxis and VTCs (see p. 129) or a *Vélib'* (see p. 125). Obviously, there are loads of posh nightclubs and discos in Paris, guarded by strict doormen who ensure that men's ties are straight and women's miniskirts are properly short. However, these days, the latest hot spots are popping up in the city's more bleakly romantic and charmingly industrial locations. Temporary bars move into abandoned factory buildings for a short time before the factories are torn down and replaced with sleek new buildings. Paris nightlife can be expensive. Cover charges for clubs and discos – depending on the establishment, day of the week and event – can easily cost 20 euros. Incidentally, many locales are closed for the month of August.

BARS

CAFÉ CHARBON (148 C3) (*∅ P6*)
The former coal merchant business from the early 19th century is an institution.

Always full. From the small ❄ terrace, you'll have a perfect view of Rue Oberkampf, which is famous for its nightlife. *Daily (Thu–Sat until 4am) | 109, rue Oberkampf | 11th arr. | tel. 01 43 57 55 13 | M 3 Parmentier | www.lecafecharbon.fr*

INSIDER TIP ► CAFÉ CHÉRI(E)
(148 C1) (*⏧ P5*)
Local pub in the hip Belleville area with lots of regulars who enjoy their drinks

CHEZ JEANNETTE
(147 E2) (*⏧ M5*)
When Jeanette was still running the show, workers and prostitutes used to stop here for a bite. Today, this bistro is a trendy hot spot. *Daily | 47, rue du Faubourg-Saint-Denis | 10th arr. | tel. 01 47 70 30 89 | M 4, 8, 9 Strasbourg-Saint-Denis | www.facebook.com/chez. jeannette*

Its name is tell-tale: Café Charbon was once a coal merchant's

alongside laid-back young Parisians. And the size of the crowds is understandable: During happy hour (5–9pm), a large beer costs just 4 euros, and if the weather cooperates, you can sip it out on the terrace. Thu–Sun from 9pm, a DJ spins tunes. The party goes on all night – or at least until the pub closes at 2 am *Closed Sun | 44, blvd. de la Villette | 19th arr. | tel. 09 53 05 93 36 | M 2, 11 Belleville | www.facebook.com/cafe. cherie*

INSIDER TIP ► ICE KUBE BAR
(149 F4) (*⏧ N3*)
Naturally, Paris also has an ice bar. No matter whether it's summer or winter, the temperature in here is a constant −10° Celsius (14° Fahrenheit). You'll be given down jackets and gloves before entering, and then you'll have your work cut out for you: You'll have exactly 25 minutes to drink three vodka cocktails and a shot (price: 26 euros). *Tue–Thu 7.30pm–midnight, Fri/Sat 7.30pm–1am | 1–5, passage Ruelle | 18th arr. | tel. 01 42 05 20 00 | M2 La Chapelle | www.kubehotel-paris.com*

LE PERCHOIR ★ ☼

For a long time, the rooftops of Paris were the exclusive preserve of the wealthy and beautiful. Then Adrien Boissaye, who took his regular smoke breaks on a rooftop terrace with a view of the Sacré-Coeur, came up with the idea to open a rooftop bar here. Parisians were soon beating down his door *(all year, changing closing days | 14, rue Crespin du Gast* (149 D3) *(Ø P7) | 11th arr. | M 2 Ménilmontant).* Which is why he also opened Perchoirs on the rooftops of the *BHV Marais* department store *(all year, changing closing days | 37, rue de la Verrerie* (147 E5) *(Ø M8) | 4th arr. | M 1, 11 Hôtel de Ville)* and the *Gare de l'Est (daily in the summer | 10, place du 11 Novembre 1918* (147 F1) *(Ø N5) | 10th arr. | M 4, 5, 7 Gare de l'Est). www.leperchoir.tv*

INSIDER TIP ▶ ROSA BONHEUR
(143 E5) *(Ø Q4)*

This hip bar in the Parc des Buttes-Chaumont (with two other locations on the Seine) has unfortunately become a victim of its own success. If you don't want to queue for hours in front of the closed park in the evening, the best thing to do is find yourself a spot in the beer garden in the afternoon, where you can fortify yourself for the full night of dancing to come. *Wed–Sun until midnight | 2, Allée de la Cascade | 19th arr. | Entrance after 8pm: large gate opposite rue Botzaris 74 | tel. 01 42 00 00 45 | M 7 Botzaris | www.rosabonheur.fr*

LE TRIBAL CAFÉ ●
(147 E1) *(Ø M5)*

A Parisian classic. The chronically skint can enjoy a free small meal here on certain days – all they have to do in return is buy a few rounds. Fair drink prices, great atmosphere. It's a fantastic deal! Wed/Thu *moules frites* (mussels with chips),

Fri/Sat couscous, each starting from 9 pm. *Closed Sun | 3, Cour des Petites Ecuries | 10th arr. | tel. 01 47 70 57 08 | M 4 Château-d'Eau*

INSIDER TIP ▶ ZÉRO ZÉRO
(148 B4) *(Ø O7)*

Tiny little bar where different DJs spin every night of the week. The walls are covered in graffiti and the atmosphere is boozy and fun. Speciality of the house: a mix of vodka and ginger named after the bar. For just 3.50 euros, it will help you forget your claustrophobia in the bar's close quarters... *Daily | 89, rue Amelot | 11th arr. | M 8 Saint-Sébastien-Froissart | www.faceook.com/pages/category/Cocktail-Bar/Zéro-Zéro-161969777215832*

MARCO POLO HIGHLIGHTS

★ **Le Batofar**
The barge on the Seine is a hot dance club → p. 86

★ **La Dame de Canton**
A musical evening on a Seine boat → p. 86

★ **Le Carmen**
Exclusive club in Belle-Époque style → p. 86

★ **Rex-Club**
Huge disco and best techno club in Paris → p. 88

★ **New Morning**
Where the world's best jazz musicians play → p. 90

★ **Le Perchoir**
The Parisians conquer the rooftops of their city → p. 85

CLUBS & DISCOS

LE BALAJO (140 B6) (*🛱 O8*)
An institution on Rue de Lappe – a street famous for its nightlife – since 1936. The tea dances held every Monday are a throwback to the club's origins: "Balajo" comes from "Bal à Jo", or "Joe's ball". During the rest of the week, there are salsa (Tue/Thu) and rock 'n' roll classes (Wed), and on weekends, you can dance to hip-hop and electro here. *Mon–Sat | 9, rue de Lappe | 11th arr. | tel. 0147000787 | M 1, 5, 8 Bastille | www.balajo.fr*

LE BATOFAR ★ (154 C5) (*🛱 P11*)
The red barge in front of the Bibliothèque Nationale de France is a popular meeting place. Experimental and techno music: very *branché*. Terrace on the deck. Quite affordable. *In 2019 re-opening after renovations, opening times see website | opposite 11, quai Francois-Mauriac | 13th arr. | tel. 0153601700 | M 6 Quai de la Gare | www.batofar.fr*

LE CARMEN ★ (140 C5) (*🛱 K4*)
If you are not a fan of snobs, avoid this club! But, if you do give it a chance, you'll be more than impressed by this former luxury brothel with its huge mirrors, tall columns and ornate ceiling. Admission is free – if you make it past the bouncer. *Tue–Sat 6pm–6am | 34, rue Duperré | 9th arr. | tel. 0145 26 50 00 | M 2 Blanche | www.le-carmen.fr*

LA CASBAH (155 D1) (*🛱 P9*)
This popular disco has an Arabian Nights flair and a restaurant. Sometimes belly dancing is offered. *Club Fri/Sat from 11.30pm, bar/restaurant Mon–Sat from 7.30pm | 18–20, rue de la Forge-Royale | 11th arr. | tel. 0143 71 04 39 | M 8 Faidherbe-Chaligny | www.casbah.fr*

LA DAME DE CANTON ★
(154 C5) (*🛱 P12*)
A real Chinese junk on the Seine! This venue is a constant on the Paris music scene: Groups like Louise Attaque, Noir Désir and Bénabar perform here. You

TOO MUCH LOVE

Proposals, honeymoons, weekends with a sweetheart – lovers from around the world travel to Paris. And how do today's global citizens symbolise their love? With a padlo... er, love lock, naturally. A heart-shaped one is best, with your initials engraved. It's easy to order online, or you can buy it from one of the dozens of street vendors on location. If even the Weir Bridge in Bakewell is overloaded with love locks, you can imagine what the situation is like in Paris. The pedestrian bridge Pont des Arts had the biggest problem – when part of the handrail collapsed under their weight, the city removed 45 tonnes of these tokens of love and replaced the latticework on the bridge with glass panels. But lovers just started hanging their locks on other bridges. Today, signs are posted prohibiting hanging locks on bridges: "Our bridges won't be able to withstand your love". The metal locks removed from the bridges were auctioned off, bringing in 250,000 euros for refugee relief.

Le Batofar: the deck-turned dance floor on the barge rocks night after night

can also enjoy a delicious meal on board before the concert starts. *Tue–Sat 7pm–midnight, bar Fri/Sat 7pm–2am | Port de la Gare | 13th arr. | tel. 0153 61 08 49 | M 6 Quai de la Gare | M 14, RER C Bibliothèque F. Mitterrand | www.damedecanton.com*

LE DIVAN DU MONDE (140 C5) (*M L4*)

The old Paris Theatre with a stage and gallery in the vibrant Pigalle district offers interesting concerts and music by DJs (Funk, Reggae, etc.). *Daily (Fri/Sat until 6am) | 75, rue des Martyrs | 18th arr. | tel. 0140 05 06 99 | M 2, 12 Pigalle | www.divandumonde.com*

FAVELA CHIC (148 B3) (*M O6*)

Dine on Brazilian cuisine and sip caipirinhas in the early evening, then dance on the benches to Latin American beats at night. *Tue–Sat (Fri/Sat until 5am) | 18, rue du Faubourg du Temple | 11th arr. | tel. 0140 21 38 14 | M 3, 5, 8, 9, 11 République | www.favelachic.com*

INSIDER TIP LE HASARD LUDIQUE

(140 B2) (*M J1*)

Another abandoned train station on the former circle line that the Parisians have reclaimed – in the truest sense of the word. Local residents helped develop the concept for the cultural centre "The Game of Chance", which opened in 2017. Regular concerts and parties are held in the ballroom, and *Cantine créative* offers a decent selection of tapas and drinks. *Tue/Wed noon–midnight, Thu–Sat noon–2am, Sun noon–10pm | 128, av. de Saint-Ouen | 18th arr. | tel. 0142 28 35 91 | M 13 Porte de Saint-Ouen | www.lehasardludique.paris*

LE QUEEN

(145 D2) (*M G6*)

The year-long No. 1 address with a gay and hetero clientele. An eclectic agenda every day. *Daily | 22, rue Quentin Bauchard | 8th arr. | tel. 0153 89 08 90 | M 1 George V | www.queen.fr*

REX-CLUB ⭐ (147 D2) (*⌂ M6*)

Huge disco under the cinema complex. Best techno club in the city, also house, disco, concerts. *Thu–Sat 11.30pm/midnight–7am | 5, bd. Poissonière | 2nd arr. | tel. 01 42 36 10 96 | M 8, 9 Bonne Nouvelle | www.rexclub.com*

SUPERSONIC (148 B6) (*⌂ O9*)

All-in-one bar, club and concert hall. The brick lofts host rock, pop, electro, and hip-hop parties. Free concerts during the week, and dancing 'til the sun comes up on weekends. *Mon–Wed 6.30pm–2am, Thu 6.30pm–4am, Fri/Sat 6.30pm–6am, Sun 6.30pm–midnight | 9, rue Biscornet | 12th arr. | tel. 01 46 28 12 90 | M 1, 5, 8 Bastille | www.facebook.com/supersonicbastille*

INSIDER TIP WANDERLUST (154 B3) (*⌂ O11*)

Club and concert hall in the futuristic neon-green Cité de la Mode directly on the Seine. It's worth a visit, especially in summer when the terrace and food court are open! *Opening times depending on season | 32, quai d'Austerlitz | 13th arr. | tel. 06 16 85 11 10 | M 5, 10, RER C Gare d'Austerlitz | www.wanderlustparis.com*

LOW BUDGET

Every Friday evening thousands of ● inline skaters congregate on a nearly 20 mile-long stretch of roads closed off to traffic. Start is at 10pm between Montparnasse station and the Montparnasse tower **(151 F3) (*⌂ H–J 10–11*)**. *Gare Montparnasse | 14th arr. | M 4, 6, 12, 13 Montparnasse-Bienvenüe | www.pari-roller.com*

Via the app and website *Mister Good Beer (www.mistergoodbeer.com)*, you can find bars with beer prices between 2 and 6 euros on the interactive map – including information about whether those are normal prices or are only valid at happy hour.

Reduced-price concert and theatre tickets are available on *www.billetreduc.com* under "Réductions". Think that's as good as it gets? Think again! Under "Invitations", you can even download free tickets for certain events.

JAZZ & LIVE MUSIC

LE BAISER SALÉ (147 E5) (*⌂ M8*)

Jazz cellar with a large bar and jazz videos. Relaxed atmosphere with salsa, blues, fusion and funk music. *Daily | 58, rue des Lombards | 1st arr. | tel. 01 42 33 37 71 | M/RER Châtelet-Les Halles | www.lebaisersale.com*

LE BATACLAN (148 B4) (*⌂ O7*)

Legendary Paris concert hall and stage that is back on its feet after the terrorist attack of 13 November 2015. The renovations took a year; now, major rock and pop acts from France and around the world are performing here regularly once again. *50, bd. Voltaire | 11th arr. | tel. 01 43 14 00 30 | M 5, 9 Oberkampf | www.le-bataclan.com*

LA BELLEVILLOISE (149 E3) (*⌂ R6*)

An old hall from the 19th century with a wonderful potpourri of activity: live concerts, art exhibitions and assorted events plus a café and restaurant. On Sundays there's a superb INSIDER TIP jazz brunch with buffet and live music. Reservation essential *(11.30am or 2pm | 29 euros)*.

The calm before the dance: It's about to get crowded and loud at Rex Club

Wed/Thu 7pm–1am, Fri 7pm–2am, Sat 11pm–2am, Sun from 5pm ball | 19–21, rue Boycr | 20th arr. | tel. 01 46 36 07 07 | M 3 Gambetta | www.labellevilloise.com

CAVEAU DE LA HUCHETTE
(147 D6) (*Ø L9*)

The old walls of a medieval vaulted cellar come to life every evening with live jazz music. *Daily | 5, rue de la Huchette | 5th arr. | tel. 01 43 26 65 05 | M 4 Saint-Michel, Cité | www.caveaudelahuchette.fr*

LE CAVERN (146 C6) (*Ø L8*)

It looks small, but it has a surprise that you can't see from the outside: At the end of the long, narrow room on the ground floor, there's a staircase leading down into a rustic vaulted cellar. Free concerts are held here regularly, and on the weekend, you can party into the wee hours of the morning. *Wed/Thu 6pm–2am, Fri/Sat 6pm–6am | 21, rue Dauphine | 6th arr. | tel. 01 43 54 53 82 | M 4, 10 Odéon | www.lecavernclub.com*

AU DUC DES LOMBARDS
(147 E5) (*Ø M8*)

Easy-going club highlighting a wide spectrum of music, from free jazz to hard bop. The restaurant (Tue–Sat) serves small meals and a daily special. *Mon–Sat | 42, rue des Lombards | 1st arr. | tel. 01 42 33 22 88 | M/RER Châtelet-Les Halles | www.ducdeslombards.com*

INSIDER TIP▶ LA GARE (143 D2) (*Ø P2*)

A new jazz club has opened in Paris! It's an ultra-cool place inside an old train station concourse. The grounds are enchantingly beautiful, with a terrace and garden. Trains haven't stopped here since 1934 – now, jazz acts large and small perform in this club. Free admission, fairly priced snacks and drinks, and excellent word-of-mouth advertising that ensures a lively, diverse crowd. *Mon–Thu 6pm–1am, Fri–Sun 6pm–2am, concerts daily from 9pm | 1, av. Corentin Cariou | 19th arr. | M 7 Corentin Cariou | www.facebook.com/LaGareJazz*

CINEMA

NEW MORNING ⭐ (147 E1) (*M5*)
The city's best and most famous jazz club where renowned international musicians take the stage. *Daily until aprrox. 1am | 7–9, rue des Petites-Ecuries | 10th arr. | tel. 01 45 23 51 41 | M 4 Château d'Eau | www.newmorning.com*

POP IN (148 B4) (*O7*)
Indie pop temple. Go inside, order a drink at the bar, head up the stairs, maybe make a little pit stop on one of the worn-out couches, then move on to the staircase at the back right of the room that leads down into the cellar, where there are free concerts every evening. *Daily | 105, rue Amelot | 11th arr. | tel. 01 48 05 56 11 | M 8 Saint-Sébastien-Froissart | www.popin.fr*

CINEMA

Foreign films, as a rule, are shown in their original language with French subtitles – *VOST (version originale avec sous-titres)* – while films dubbed into French are denoted as *v. f. (version française)*.
In addition to the three major chains *Gaumont Pathé (www.cinemasgaumont pathe.com)*, *UGC (www.ugc.fr)* and *MK2 (www.mk2.com)*, the city offers many small, independent cinemas.

CINÉMATHÈQUE FRANÇAISE (155 D4) (*P11*)
The futuristic building by Frank O. Gehry is a mecca for film freaks! A museum *(Wed–Mon noon–7pm | admission 5 euros)* with film posters, costumes and props, an archive with more than 40,000 films and half a million photos, and multiple cinemas. Film history comes to life here. Online calendar with all film showtimes. *Closed Tue | 51, rue de Bercy | 12th arr. | M 6, 14 Bercy | www. cinematheque.fr*

CONCERTS

A number of stages showcase all types of music by top performers and amateurs alike. The city is also an important venue for ethnic music from all over the world. Especially during the summer, there are many free events and musicians often play in the parks in July/August.

LA CIGALE (140 C5) (*L4*)
International stars have performed at this venue, including Kevin Costner and his band, Modern West. *120, bd. Rochechouart | 18th arr. | tel. 01 49 25 89 99 | M 2, 12 Pigalle | www.lacigale.fr*

OLYMPIA (145 B2) (*J6*)
Legendary, world-famous concert hall since the 19th century hosting performers ranging from French celebrities to the Rolling Stones. *28, bd. des Capucines | 9th arr. | tel. 08 92 68 33 68 (*) | M 3, 7, 8 Opéra | RER A Auber | www.olympiahall.com*

PHILHARMONIE DE PARIS (151 F3) (*R2*)
Construction on the philharmonic hall designed by Jean Novel with its spectacular architecture including an accessible roof was completed in 2015. None of the over 2,400 seats is more than 30 m (33 yds) from the stage in the middle. The repertoire ranges from classic to world music and there is a café and a 🍽 panorama restaurant. *221, av. Jean-Jaurès | 19th arr. | tel. 01 44 84 44 84 | M 5 Porte de Pantin | www.philharmoniedeparis.fr*

LE ZÉNITH (143 E2) (*R2*)
This huge concert hall in the Parc de la Villette is a venue for rock and pop concerts accomodating up to 9,000 fans. *211, av. Jean-Jaurès | 19th arr. | tel. 01 44 52 54 56 | M 5 Porte de Pantin | www.lezenith.com*

REVUES

LE CRAZY HORSE (144 C3) *(ₘ F6)*
Eroticism paired with artistic sensibility. A combination of ballet and striptease with beautiful aesthetic effects. *Shows: Sun–Fri 8.15pm, 10.45pm, Sat 7pm,*

THEATRE

You'd like to go to the theatre, but don't speak a word of French? *Theatre in Paris (www.theatreinparis.com)* has the answer: English surtitles! All available shows are listed on the website.

Crazy Horse: striptease with a twist – an imaginative combination of the erotic and aesthetic

9.30pm, 11.45pm | from 65 euros | 12, av. George V | 8th arr. | tel. 01 47 23 32 32 | M 1 George V | M 9 Alma Marceau | www. lecrazyhorseparis.com

LE MOULIN ROUGE (140 B4) *(ₘ K3)*
Lavish revues in the "red mill" immortalised by Henri de Toulouse-Lautrec and the birthplace of the cancan, located at the foot of Montmartre. *Shows between 1pm and 11pm | from 102 euros (from 112 euros including half a bottle of champagne, from 165 euros including lunch, from 190 euros including dinner) | 82, bd. de Clichy | 18th arr. | tel. 01 53 09 82 82 | M 2 Blanche | www. moulinrouge.fr*

COMÉDIE FRANÇAISE (146 C4) *(ₘ K7)*
Founded in 1680 under Louis XIV. Classic theatre in the tradition of Molière. ● Seats with an obstructed view are available an hour before the show for just 5 euros; on the first Monday of the month, everyone under 28 can attend for free. *1, place Colette | 1st arr. | tel. 01 44 58 15 15 | M 1, 7 Palais Royal–Musée du Louvre | www.comedie-francaise.fr*

THÉÂTRE DE LA VILLE (147 D5) *(ₘ L8)*
Premier stage in Paris for modern dance, also dramatic works and music (especially ethnic). *2, pl. du Châtelet | 4th arr. | tel. 01 42 74 22 77 | M/RER Châtelet-Les Halles |www.theatredelaville-paris.com*

WHERE TO STAY

As one of the most important tourist spots worldwide, Paris has an extensive range of accommodation in every category.

In addition to the globally recognised hotel palaces such as the Plaza Athénée, which are synonymous with luxury and sophistication, there are also real jewels among the more reasonable, modest establishments; you just have to know where to find them. Many offer authentic charm, an informal atmosphere and are lovingly maintained. These addresses, as well as certain luxury hotels, are booked up quickly from April to July, as well as in September and October. It is advisable to reserve your hotel of choice well in advance. If you're pressed for time, the *Office du Tourisme* (see p. 126) can lend a hand. Hotel reservations can also be made at: *www.leshotelsde paris.com.*

The hotel category (one to four stars) is shown on hotel signs. Note, however, there are also hotels that are not classified, and the number of stars is not always indicative of the amenities provided.

Most places demand written confirmation by e-mail, fax, letter or a voucher. A credit card number or a deposit is also often required. Cancellations must be made in writing. Rates tend to vary according to the season and, as a rule, room prices quoted in brochures and price lists apply to a double room without breakfast. In Paris, a nominal visitor's tax is charged. To avoid misun-

Photo: Rolls-Royce in front of the Hôtel George V

Bonne nuit: There's no shortage of beds in Paris. From low budget to luxury – the choice is yours!

derstandings, check the price list beforehand which has to be clearly displayed at the hotel entrance.

HOTELS: EXPENSIVE

FOUR SEASONS GEORGE V
(144 C2) (*∅ F6*)

After extensive restorations in the 18th-century style, this prestigious address is more radiant than ever with its generously sized, luxurious rooms and *Le Cinq*, Philippe Legendre's two-star restaurant. *185 rooms, 58 apartments | 31, av. George V | 8th arr. | tel. 01 49 52 70 00 | M 1 George V | www.fourseasons.com/paris*

L'HÔTEL ★ ● (146 C5) (*∅ K8*)

Highly distinguished but nevertheless quite cosy, and more beautiful than ever following its tasteful renovations by the famous designer Jacques Garcia. Even the renowned writer Oscar Wilde, who died here in 1900 in suite no. 13, appreciated the hotel's comfort. Unique round atrium. Large rooms in the Baroque, Empire, Art Deco or Japanese style. The vaulted cellar has a swimming pool and hamam reminiscent of a Roman spa. Incredible Michelin-star restaurant (*Le Bélier, see p. 63*). *15 rooms, 4 suites, 1 apartment | 13, rue des Beaux*

The cosy hotel with the famous name is *très charmant*

Arts | 6th arr. | tel. 01 44 41 99 00 | M 4 Saint-Germain-des-Prés | www.l-hotel. com

K+K HOTEL CAYRÉ (146 A5) (*Ⓜ J10*)
This boutique hotel combines exceptional comfort and modern design. The chain maintains an excellent standard at attractive prices. In Paris, the hotel is optimally located in Saint-Germain-des-Prés. *125 rooms and suites | 4, bd. Raspail | 7th arr. | tel. 01 45 44 38 88 | M 12 Rue du Bac | www.kkhotels.com/ cayre*

PAVILLON DE LA REINE
(148 B5) (*Ⓜ O8*)
You'll feel very regal when you pass through the arcades to the former royal square, the Place des Vosges, leaving the hectic Marais district behind you as you enter this peaceful oasis with its lush courtyard. The spa is utterly relaxing. *33 rooms, 21 suites | 28, pl. des Vosges | 3rd arr. | tel. 01 40 29 19 19 | M 1, 5, 8 Bastille | www.pavillon-de-la-reine.com*

TERRASS" HÔTEL ☆ (148 B4) (*Ⓜ K3*)
This hotel lies at the foot of Montmarte. It owes its name to its 1,500 square-foot rooftop terrace offering a truly fantastic view over the entire city. All 92 rooms were stylishly renovated in 2015. *12–14, rue Joseph de Maistre | 18th arr. | tel. 01 46 06 72 85 | M 12 Abbesses | www. terrass-hotel.com*

HOTELS: MODERATE

HÔTEL DES ARTS (147 D2) (*Ⓜ L5*)
Charming and lovely small hotel in a quiet yet central location with spacious rooms. *25 rooms | 7, cité Bergère | 9th arr. | tel. 01 42 46 73 30 | M 8, 9 Grands Boulevards | www.hoteldesarts.fr*

HÔTEL ARVOR SAINT GEORGES
(140 C6) (*Ⓜ K4*)
Well maintained, renovated hotel in a quiet neighbourhood. Modern design. Not far from the Gare du Nord, Montmartre and major department stores. *24 rooms, 6 suites | 8, rue Laferrière |*

9th arr. | tel. 01 48 78 60 92 | M 12 Saint-Georges | hotelarvor.com

HÔTEL DE L'AVRE
(150 C2) (*m F9*)

This small hotel near the École Militaire is full of charm. The pastel-coloured rooms have all been designed with the utmost care. In summer you can have breakfast in the lovely courtyard garden. *26 rooms | 21, rue de l'Avre | 15th arr. | tel. 01 45 75 31 03 | M 6, 8, 10 La Motte-Picquet Grenelle | www.hotel delavre.com*

HÔTEL CHOPIN (147 D2) (*m L6*)

Small, but charming hotel in a beautiful 19th-century building at the end of the lovely Passage Jouffroy. Pleasantly quiet. *36 rooms | 46,Passage Jouffroy | 9th arr. | tel. 01 47 70 58 10 | M 8, 9 Grands Boulevards | www.hotelchopin.fr*

HÔTEL DU COLLÈGE DE FRANCE
(153 D1) (*m L9*)

This cosy and well-run hotel is situated in the centre of the hectic Quartier Latin in a surprisingly quiet location. *29 rooms | 7, rue Thénard | 5th arr. | tel. 01 43 26 78 36 | M 10 Maubert-Mutualité | www.hotel-collegedefrance.com*

HÔTEL DES GRANDES ECOLES ★
(153 E2) (*m M9*)

An absolute highlight. Who would expect a country house with park-like grounds only a stone's throw from the vibrant rue Mouffetard and Panthéon? Each room in the three small buildings is decorated with period furniture. Most rooms have a view of the garden where you can enjoy breakfast in this peaceful setting. *51 rooms | 75, rue du Cardinal Lemoine | 5th arr. | tel. 01 43 26 79 23 | M 10 Cardinal Lemoine | www.hotel-grandes-ecoles.com*

HÔTEL LANGLOIS ★
(140 C6) (*m K5*)

A real gem. The elegant entrance hall decorated with marble and wood lives up to its promise. The 25 rooms (one with three beds) and two suites are individually furnished with original Art Deco and Art Nouveau furniture. View of Sacré-Cœur from the very top. Fireplace in each room. *63, rue Saint-Lazare | 9th arr. | tel. 01 48 74 78 24 | M 12 Trinité d'Estienne d'Orves | www.hotel-langlois.com*

HÔTEL MOLIÈRE
(146 C3) (*m K7*)

This enchanting hotel is located on the street where the great playwright was born in 1622 and is only steps away from the Palais Royal. It is no surprise that

---

MARCO POLO HIGHLIGHTS

★ **L'Hôtel**
This jewel offers the most exclusive rooms and a pool in a vaulted cellar → **p. 93**

★ **Hôtel des Grandes Ecoles**
A country house and garden in the heart of Paris → **p. 95**

★ **Hôtel Langlois**
Marble busts and Art Deco, Art Nouveau and a fireplace in every room → **p. 95**

★ **Hôtel de Nesle**
Oasis of calm in lively Saint-Germain-des-Prés → **p. 98**

★ **Nouvel Hôtel**
Cosy and cheerful with a Provence-style garden → **p. 98**

the hotel exudes Old French elegance. *29 rooms | 21, rue Molière | 1st arr. | tel. 01 42 96 22 01 | M 1 Palais Royal-Musée du Louvre | www.hotel-moliere.fr*

LE RELAIS DU MARAIS
(147 F3) *(🗺 N6)*
Two-star hotel with elegant furnishings in the middle of Marais. Close to the best places for shopping. Unusually large breakfast buffet. *37 rooms | 76, rue Turbigo | 3rd arr. | tel. 01 42 72 78 88 | M 3 Temple | www.hotel-paris-relaisdumarais.com*

HÔTEL SAINT-CHARLES
(153 E6) *(🗺 M12)*
Very attractive designer hotel in the heart of the lively nightlife district Butte-aux-Cailles. Pleasantly calm despite its location and with a nice atmosphere. *57 rooms | 6, rue de l'Espérance | 13th arr. | tel. 01 45 89 56 54 | M 6 Corvisart, M 5, 6, 7 Place d'Italie | www.hotel-saint-charles.com*

HÔTEL SAINT-MERRY
(147 E5) *(🗺 M8)*
Unconventional hotel that was once part of a Gothic chapel and now furnished accordingly. Its location between Les Halles and Marais is ideal for tourists. *11 rooms, 1 suite | 78, rue de la Verrerie | 4th arr. | tel. 01 42 78 14 15 | M 1, 11 Hôtel de Ville | www.saintmerrymarais.com*

MORE THAN A GOOD NIGHT'S SLEEP

Water beds
In the thick of it all, and still secluded: There are countless *houseboats* on the Seine, known as *péniches* in French. Staying in one isn't exactly cheap, but it's worth the price! From the Seine, you'll have a view of the city that's almost too clichéd to be real. The owners of the houseboats are among the privileged few Parisians who have a terrace. It's wonderful, especially when the weather cooperates. Many boat owners offer their floating homes to let on *Airbnb.* You can find other houseboats on the website of French start-up *Boatyng (www.boatyng.com),* which applies the concept of Airbnb to accommodations on the water. *Expensive*

Down by the river (154 B3) ***(🗺 O11)***
The first Parisian hotel on the Seine. Stylish, modern, with lots of metal, glass and wood, on the bank in front of the Gare d'Austerlitz, a hip area. When it comes to the rooms, you have a choice between a view of the pier or the Seine. If you want something extra-special, why not reserve the golden-orange designer suite "Sunset", where the décor makes it feel like it's always sundown? If *OFF Paris Seine* is too expensive for you, you might want to just stop by for a drink: At 4.30pm, all hotel guests have to leave the pool, because from 6pm to midnight, the ship's bar is open to the public, serving INSIDER TIP cocktails and tapas for everyone. *54 rooms, 4 suites | 20–22, Port d'Austerlitz | 13th arr | tel. 01 44 06 62 65 | M 5, 10, RER C Gare d'Austerlitz | www.offparisseine.com | Expensive*

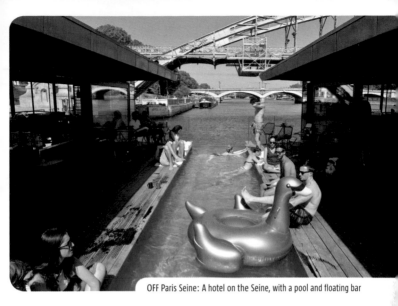

OFF Paris Seine: A hotel on the Seine, with a pool and floating bar

HOTELS: BUDGET

HÔTEL DES ARTS-MONTMARTRE
(140 C4) (*K3*)

Renoir painted his famous painting, *Moulin de la Galette,* only a few feet from here. The cosy hotel is located on a quiet lane that winds up Montmartre. The 50 rooms are tastefully furnished. Surprisingly affordable for a three-star hotel. *5, rue Tholozé | 18th arr. | tel. 01 46 06 30 52 | M 2 Blanche | www.arts-hotel-paris.com*

INSIDER TIP HÔTEL ELDORADO
(140 A4) (*J3*)

A real treasure with a lovely garden at the centre of Paris with tastefully furnished rooms. Quiet, but centrally located at the foot of Montmartre. Great wine bar and restaurant with a summer terrace, cuisine with a Mediterranean flair. *33 rooms | 18, rue des Dames | 17th arr. | tel. 01 45 22 35 21 | M 2, 13 Place de Clichy | eldoradohotel.fr*

ERMITAGE SACRÉ-CŒUR
(141 D4) (*L3*)

This very pretty romantic little hotel in a beautiful palais from the time of Napoleon III is located in the middle of the Montmatre quarter. Tranquil with a great view of the city. Breakfast is included. *3 rooms, 3 apt. | 24, rue Lamarck | 18th arr. | tel. 01 42 64 79 22 | M 4 Château Rouge | www.ermitagesacrecoeur.fr*

HÔTEL JARDIN DE VILLIERS
(139 E5) (*H3*)

Pleasant small hotel with – as its name suggests – an attractive garden where you can enjoy breakfast. On rainy days the veranda provides a suitable alternative. Not far from the main attractions. Fitness room. The rooms are quite modern and tastefully furnished. *26 rooms | 18, rue Claude Poulillet | 17th arr. | tel. 01 42 67 15 60 | M 2, 3 Villiers | www.jardindevilliers.com*

The inviting Hôtel de Nesle: A promising outlook for a comfortable night

HÔTEL DE NESLE ★
(146 C6) (*L8*)

You'll be transported into another world as soon as you see the entrance hall with its flea market treasures. The romantic rooms are decorated very individually, each one different. All rooms have showers, but 9 don't have an en-suite toilet (communal toilet in the hall). There is even a Moroccan room INSIDERTIP (with a real hamam), an Egyptian, a Provençal and an African room. Exquisite garden with sculptures and terrace. *18 rooms | 7, rue de Nesle | 6th arr. | tel. 0143546241 | M 4, 10 Odéon | www.hoteldenesleparis.com*

NOUVEL HÔTEL ★
(155 F2) (*R10*)

Lovingly furnished, very quiet and clean rooms with Laura Ashley décor. Each room has a refurbished bathroom and a TV. Informal atmosphere. The small Provence-inspired courtyard and beautiful, luxuriant garden of wild vines and bamboo is the ideal place to relax. Room 109 with its direct access to the garden is extremely popular. Two family rooms and a three-bed room are also available. *27 rooms | 24, av. du Bel-Air | 12th arr. | tel. 0143430181 | M 1, 2, 6, 9, RER A Nation | www.nouvel-hotel-paris. com*

HÔTEL PRATIC
(148 A6) (*N8*)

Well-looked after, quaint hotel with charm and old furniture at the heart of the Marais district and close to Place des Vosges. *23 rooms | 9, rue d'Ormesson | 4th arr. | tel. 0148878047 | M 1 Saint-Paul | www.pratichotelparis.com*

HÔTEL DU PRINTEMPS
(155 F2) (*R10*)

Well-kept, quiet, good-value hotel that has recently been tastefully renovated. Rooms with four beds available for families. *38 rooms | 80, bd. de Picpus | 12th arr. | tel. 01 43 43 62 31 | M 6 Picpus | www.hotel-paris-printemps.com*

SOLAR HÔTEL ⊙
(152 B5) *(𝄞 J12)*

The Solar is the first hotel in Paris to call itself ecological and not only publicly divulges how much energy it uses, but also endeavours to reduce this figure. Breakfast is 100% organic. Nobody will mind if you bring your own food to eat in the garden. True to form, bicycles are at your disposal for exploring the city. *24 rooms | 22, rue Boulard | 14th arr. | tel. 01 43 21 08 20 | M 4, 6, RER B Denfert Rochereau | www.solarhotel.fr*

BED & BREAKFAST

You want to get to know the city, but you also want to meet Julie, François and Joëlle? No problem! Many Parisians offer their guest rooms to travellers. On *www.bed-and-breakfast-in-paris.com*, you will find a selection of rooms lovingly compiled by Françoise Foret, who liaises between the guests and her countrymen on location.

YOUTH HOSTELS

AUBERGE DE JEUNESSE ADVENIAT
(145 D2) *(𝄞 G6)*

Christian hospitality, at affordable prices and in a great location, garnished with a helping of brotherly love. Upon request, this hostel will connect you with a French family for dinner, or arrange for you to spend an afternoon at a charitable organisation that cares for Paris's homeless. *Membership card 5 euros. Closed between 11am and 4pm. 10, rue François-1er | 8th arr. | tel. 01 77 45 89 10 | M 1, M 13 Champs-Elysées-Clemenceau | www.adveniat-paris.org*

AUBERGES DE JEUNESSE PARIS – YVES ROBERT ⊙ (150 A4) *(𝄞 N3)*

This tastefully-furnished and environmentally-friendly hostel, outfitted with solar panels on the roof, is one of three Paris hostels of the Hostelling International network. The former railway station halls have been converted into 103 rooms with 330 beds. The price per person in a dorm is under 30 euros, in a double room 68 euros per person. Older individuals and families are also welcome. A hostel card (11 euros) is a must. As an added bonus, Gare du Nord and Gare de 'Est are in walking distance. *20, Esplanade Nathalie Sarraute | 18th arr. |*

LOW BUDGET

Maisons Internationales de Jeunesse et des Etudiants, MIJE (tel. 01 42 74 23 45 | www.mije.com) runs three outstanding youth hostels in beautifully renovated city palais from the 16th and 17th century in the middle of the Marais district in the 4th arrondissement **(147 F6)** *(𝄞 N8)*. They are located at *6, rue de Fourcy (M 1 Saint-Paul), 11, rue du Fauconnier (M 1 Saint-Paul)* and *12, rue des Barres (M 1, 11 Hôtel de Ville)*. Guests can enjoy an inexpensive meal in the adjoining restaurant on rue de Fourcy.

One of the cheapest hotels in the centre of Paris is the *Hôtel Tiquetonne* **(147 E3)** *(𝄞 L7)* *(48 rooms | 6, rue Tiquetonne | 2nd arr. | tel. 01 42 36 94 58 | M 4 Etienne Marcel | www.hoteltiquetonne.fr)*. Quiet location (pedestrian zone) in the lively quarter around Les Halles. Great value for money.

tel. 0140 38 87 90 | M 12 Marx Dormoy | www.hifrance.org

INSIDER TIP ▶ OOPS! HOSTEL
(153 E5) (🌀 M12)

Trendy design hotel for young people on a budget (room from 70 euros, bed in a dorm from 27 euros per person). Great location for exploring Paris with a Vélib station right in front of the entrance. Five minutes from rue Mouffetard. *47 double and shared rooms | 50, av. des Gobelins | 13th arr. | tel. 0147 07 47 00 | M 7 Les Gobelins | www.oops-paris.com*

LES PIAULES **(148 C2) (🌀 P6)**

Before Matthieu, Damien and Louis founded their own hostel in 2015 – with 162 beds in the hip northeast of Paris – they backpacked around the world themselves. Their travel experience helped them design the perfect bunk beds, with curtains, lockers and power sockets for charging mobile phones at night. The bar serves local products, the 🌿 rooftop terrace offers a fantastic view of the city – and all of this comes at an affordable price. A night in a shared dormitory costs between 30 and 40 euros. *59, blvd. de Belleville | 11th arr. | tel. 0143 55 09 97 | M 2 Couronnes | www.lespiaules.com*

3 DUCKS HOSTEL **(150 B3) (🌀 E10)**

This hostel advertises itself as a "10-minute walk from the Eiffel Tower" – that might be a bit optimistic, but you should manage the walk within 20 minutes. The hostel was renovated from the ground up in 2016; it's located in a middle-class residential neighbourhood. The 19 rooms are painted in bright colours and fun designs. A double room costs just under 100 euros per night; a bed in a dorm will run you less than 30 euros. *6, Place Etienne Pernet | 15th arr. | tel. 0148 42 04 05 | M 8 Félix Faure | www.3ducks.fr*

FLATS

Naturally, lots of Parisians let rooms in their homes via *(www.airbnb.com)*. The

SPOTLIGHT ON SPORTS

Boule sports – No, really, "boules" actually is a sport! And it's a quintessentially French one, at that. Pensioners and wealthy espadrilles-wearing retirees in the south of France aren't the only ones who play – in fact, in Paris, meeting for a game of boules in the summer is the hip new trend. *Bouldrome* **(157 F5) (🌀 R–S12)** *(Route des Fortifications | M 8 Porte de Charenton)* in the 12th arrondissement, for example, organises tournaments and even hosts boules parties with open-air bars and DJs *(www.facebook.com/lesaperosdelapetanque).*

Horsemanship – At the *Théâtre Équestre Zingaro* **(157 F1) (🌀 O)** *(176, av. Jean Jaurès | www.bartabas.fr/theatre-zingaro | M 7 Fort d'Aubervilliers)* – the Equestrian Theatre Zingaro in English – run by equestrian choreographer Bartabas in Aubervilliers offers equestrian sports with a flair for the artistic. Bartabas heads the riding academy, which is also located in the royal stables of the palace of Versailles (see p. 58) and can be viewed separately *(www.bartabas.fr/academie-equestre-de-versailles).*

Graffiti points the way to the Auberge de Jeunesse Paris – Yves Robert

city has placed tight restrictions on the letting of holiday flats, but you will still find thousands of flats in all price categories available in the city. If you'd like personal assistance in finding a holiday rental, try: *www.citycosy.com.* And on *www.we-paris.com,* you can reserve flats that come with a full fridge.

CHEZ BERTRAND
(140 C2) *(ꝏ L1)*

Totally bonkers! In this hotel, you might find your toilet in a disused telephone booth. The chandelier is made of tennis balls, the bed is inside an old Citroën, and you can eat a meal off the loading bed of a minivan. The five motley holiday flats managed by Bertrand de Neuville are all located in the north of the city, not far from Montmartre and the Saint-Ouen

flea market. Prices start at 170 euros for two nights. *12, rue Gustave Rouanet | 18th arr. | tel. 06 63 19 19 87 | M 4 Porte de Clignancourt | www.chezbertrand.com, www.paris-champion.de, www.paris-circus.com*

LOFT PARIS
(140 B4) *(ꝏ K3)*

Five well-equipped large flats as well as a suite situated on a very quiet side street in the middle of Montmartre. Some have a small private courtyard and are furnished with period pieces. Each can accommodate up to six guests – ideal for families, groups or couples. *7, cité Véron | 18th arr. | tel. 06 14 48 47 48 | M 2 Blanche | www.loft-paris.fr*

DISCOVERY TOURS

① PARIS AT A GLANCE

START: ① Fouquet's
END: ⑩ Caveau de la Huchette

Distance:
➡ 27.5 km/17 miles

1 day
Walking time
(without stops)
3 hours

COSTS: Métro/bus tickets 8 euros, Batobus ticket 17 euros, admission for the Musée d'Orsay and the Arc de Triomphe 12 euros each

IMPORTANT TIPS: the nearest Métro station to the start of the tour on the Champs-Elysées is M 1 George V
Reserve a table for dinner at ⑨ **Bouillon Racine** ahead!
The nearest Métro stations to the last stop on the tour on rue de la Huche are M 4 Saint-Michel or Cité.

Would you like to explore the places that are unique to this city? Then the Discovery Tours are just the thing for you – they include terrific tips for stops worth making, breathtaking places to visit, selected restaurants and fun activities. It's even easier with the Touring App: download the tour with map and route to your smartphone using the QR Code on pages 2/3 or from the website address in the footer below – and you'll never get lost again even when you're offline.

TOURING APP

→ p. 2/3

With a diameter of approx. 5 km (3.1 miles), the core of the city is smaller than one might expect. You can get a good feel for the metropolis on the water, but the view from the Arc de Triomphe will also help you get your bearings. No visit to Paris would be complete without a stop at the Eiffel Tower and the Louvre, but some of the best art awaits at the Musée d'Orsay. A meal in an Art Nouveau-style restaurant followed by a walk through the lighted streets of Paris cap off the experience.

09:00am Start your day with breakfast on the **Champs-Elysées** → p. 35. One of the most famous of the many street cafés is **❶ Fouquet's** (daily | no. 99 | 8th arr. | tel.

❶ Fouquet's ☕

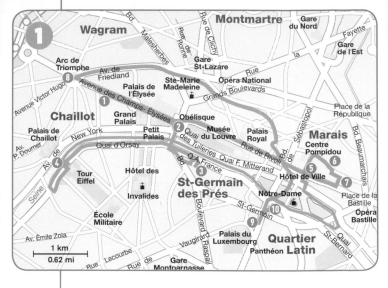

0140 69 60 50 | Expensive). Film stars celebrate the annual César awards here. The hustle and bustle along this boulevard with the Arc de Triomphe in the background is a fitting start for a walk through Paris.

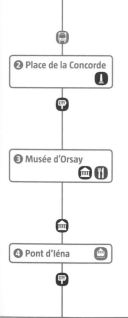

② Place de la Concorde

③ Musée d'Orsay

④ Pont d'Iéna

10:00am **Ride down this impressive avenue on a no. 73 bus,** passing by the glass-roofed Grand Palais and the Petit Palais → p. 36. As you cross **② Place de la Concorde** → p. 40 with its stately obelisk and gigantic monumental fountains, you will get a feel for the enormity of this square. **Before the bus turns,** make sure to take a look at the Jardin des Tuileries → p. 36, the oldest park in the city. It links the square with the Louvre complex. After the bus crosses the Seine, **get off at the stop in front of the ③ Musée d'Orsay → p. 39.** You will surely be delighted by the tasteful architecture of this converted railway station and the sizeable collection of French Impressionist art that it holds. After a snack at the museum, **take the RER C from the Musée d'Orsay station for three stops to the** Eiffel Tower → p. 29.

01:00pm At the foot of this landmark, **on the ④ Pont d'Iéna bridge, the boats belonging to the Batobus line dock**. Hop aboard and get to know the city from an entirely new perspective on the Seine. During the trip, the boat glides beneath a number of bridges, including the gilded **Pont Alexandre III** → **p. 40** and the famous **Pont Neuf** → **p. 52** – bringing you to the heart of the city, the islands on the Seine. The long walls of the former royal seat known as the Louvre → p. 37, now the largest museum in the world, stretch along the left-hand side. As the boat circles the islands, you will also be able to admire the Gothic spires of **Notre Dame Cathedral**→ **p. 51**.

`02:00pm` Disembark at the ❺ **Hôtel de Ville** → **p. 46** stop. Walk from here along **rue de Rivoli and rue Vieille du Temple** to the nearby bustling district of ❻ **Marais** → **p. 72**. Check out the numerous small shops such as a branch of the **Uniqlo** chain on rue des Francs-Bourgeois (no. 39) with its inexpensive fashion collections. Then take a break in one of the nostalgic cafés in this quarter. A favourite spot on the impressive former royal square, the **Place des Vosges** → **p. 48**, is ❼ **Café Hugo** (daily | no. 22 | 4th arr. | tel. 01 42 72 64 04 | Budget–Moderate).

`05:00pm` Head down to the Métro **at the Saint Paul station. Walk down rue de Birague and rue Saint-Antoine to get to the station and then take the M1 to Charles de Gaulle-Étoile.** This underground route will bring you back to the starting point of the tour and just a bit further to the ❽ **Arc de Triomphe** → **p. 34** and its viewing platform. Twelve avenues converge like a star (étoile) at Place Charles de Gaulle-Étoile, offering the best overview of the layout of the city. By now, you'll surely be ready for diner and you'll hopefully have booked a table at one of the classic Belle-Époque restaurants for which Paris is so well-known.

`08:00pm` A particularly good address is ❾ **Bouillon Racine** → **p. 65** in the old intellectual neighbourhood of Saint-Germain-des-Prés → p. 106. For the fastest way to get there, **take the RER A from Charles de Gaulle-Étoile and change trains Châtelet-Les Halles to the RER B and get off at Saint-Michel.** The floral designs so typical of the Art Nouveau style cloak the restaurant whose menu is likewise decorative. Enjoy a leisurely meal before delving into the lively nightlife in this area. End the day in true Parisian style at one of the most authentic jazz clubs in the district, ❿ **Caveau de la Huchette** → **p. 89**.

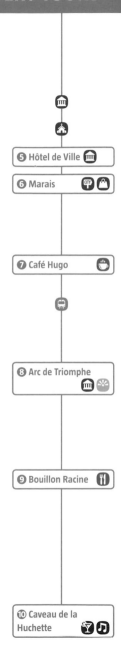

❺ Hôtel de Ville

❻ Marais

❼ Café Hugo

❽ Arc de Triomphe

❾ Bouillon Racine

❿ Caveau de la Huchette

2 THE INTELLECTUAL HEART OF PARIS

START: ❶ Les Deux Magots
END: ❿ Café Maure

4 hours
Walking time
(without stops)
1¼ hours

Distance:
➡ 4.8 km/3 miles

IMPORTANT TIPS: the nearest Métro station to the start of the tour on Place Saint-Germain-des-Prés is M 4 Saint-Germain-des-Prés
The nearest Métro stations to the last stop on the tour on rue Geoffrey Saint-Hilaire are M 7 Place Monge or Censier Daubenton

Whereas the right bank *(rive droite)* had long been the place where money was made and spent, the left bank *(rive gauche)* around ★ Saint-Germain-des-Prés and the Quartier Latin was the home of the intellectual scene. In the 1930s and 1950s, much philosophising went on at Café Flore, Les Deux Magots or in the Jardin du Luxembourg. The art academy and university still radiate over this area today, and the free spirit of this tradition lives on. Bask in this inspiration as you walk through the left bank!

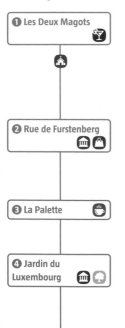

❶ Les Deux Magots

❷ Rue de Furstenberg

❸ La Palette

❹ Jardin du Luxembourg

The patio of ❶ **Les Deux Magots** → p. 63 is a bit like a box at the theatre, making it the perfect place to start this tour. Sit back and relax as you watch people stroll past. The church Saint-Germain-des-Prés, one of the oldest in Paris, is just opposite. Rue Bonaparte, as well as the other streets in this area, are full of galleries, antique dealers, fabric shops, cafés and restaurants. **Follow rue de l'Abbaye behind the church** to the romantic, tree-lined square on ❷ **Rue de Furstenberg**, which was once home to the studio of the artist Eugène Delacroix (no. 6) – which you can visit for free if you've bought a ticket for the Louvre *(www.musee-delacroix.fr).* **Then turn right down rue Jacob, which leads to the lively rue de Seine.** Stop for coffee on the patio of the ever-popular ❸ **La Palette** *(daily | 43, Rue de Seine | tel. 01 43 26 68 15).* **Continue along rue Jacques Callot, then turn right up rue Mazarine, and head over Boulevard Saint-Germain to rue de l'Odéon.** Walk past the neoclassical Théâtre de l'Odéon until you come to the ❹ **Jardin du Luxembourg** → p. 50, one of the most popular parks in Paris. Take in the Palais du Luxembourg, modelled after the Florentine Palazzo Pitti, as you sit on the edge of the pond or the shaded **Fontaine de Médicis**.

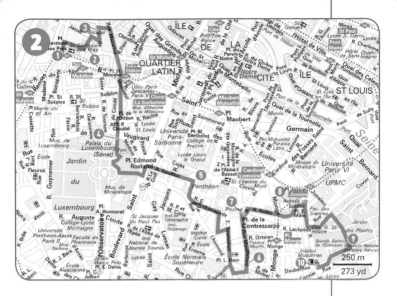

Across from the main entrance, on the other side of the lively Boulevard Saint-Michel with its street cafés, **follow rue Soufflot** up to the domed **⑤ Panthéon → p. 52**, a mausoleum in which many French luminaries are buried. The narrow lanes that wind up the Montagne Sainte-Geneviève are part of one of the oldest neighbourhoods in Paris.

Walk along rue Malebranche, rue des Fossés Saint-Jacques, which runs through the trench around a medieval city wall, and – after crossing the Place de l'Estrapade with its trees, benches and a fountain – **rue de l'Estrapade.** These streets exude a tranquillity reminiscent of a provincial town. Thanks to the nearby Sorbonne university and some of the most elite schools in the country, this area is an important centre of intellectual life in the city. **Stroll down rue Laromiguière, rue Amyot and rue Tournefort to rue Lohmond and then turn left into the narrow Passage des Postes,** which is noticeably livelier.

A colourful market with many excellent grocers is situated on the lower end of the very old, yet always bustling **⑥ Rue Mouffetard → p. 53.** The upper end of the "Mouff" definitely caters more to tourists. But, the food

Fresh seafood of all kinds at a fishmonger's on rue Mouffetard

⑦ Place de la Contrescarpe 🅟

⑧ Arènes de Lutèce 🏛

⑨ Jardin des Plantes 🌳

⑩ Café Maure 🕌 🍴

stall **Au p'tit Grec** at no. 66 sells the moistest crépes and galettes in Paris. Eat your crépe at the upper end of street on **⑦ Place de la Contrescarpe**, where street musicians and free massages ensure for a moment of relaxation (of course, the nice people offering the massages appreciate it if you give them a tip).

From rue du Cardinal Lemoine (Ernest Hemingway once lived at no. 74), **walk down rue Rollin** with its old, crooked houses. **Go down the steps and across rue Monge** to the **⑧ Arènes de Lutèce**, a Roman amphitheatre, on the left-hand side, which was first excavated in the 19th century. Today it is a popular haunt among teenagers. **Head right down rue Linné** (which turns into rue Geoffroy Saint-Hilaire) and go to the **⑨ Jardin des Plantes** → p. 119 with its gardens, greenhouses and the Muséum National d'Histoire Naturelle → p. 119. **Continue along rue Buffon and rue Daubenton to the Grande Mosquée de Paris**. Delve into an Arabian world at the end of your stroll: with mint tea and sweet honey pastries in the tea room at **⑩ Café Maure** *(daily | rue Geoffroy St-Hilaire 39 | 5th arr. | tel. 0143311432 | www.la-*

mosquee.com | Budget) within the complex of the grand mosque.

IN THE FOOTSTEPS OF THE ARTISTS OF MONTMARTRE

START: ❶ Moulin Rouge
END: ⓫ L'atelier Montmartre

3 hours
Walking time
(without stops)
40 minutes

Distance:
➡ 2.4 km/1.5 miles

IMPORTANT TIPS: The nearest Métro station to the start of the tour is M 2 Blanche; the nearest Métro station to the last stop on the tour on rue Burg is M 12 Abbesses.

★ Montmartre is known as the cradle of modern art. Artists from all over Europe migrated to what was then just a small village on this hill at the turn of the 20th century. As you walk through this district today, you can easily imagine how simple artists, whose works often now hang in the great museums of Paris, went about their daily lives.

The sex trade flourishes around the Métro station Blanche near the ❶ **Moulin Rouge** → p. 91, which is still a favourite tourist attraction. Leave this slightly shabby area behind and **walk up the hill via rue Lépic.** Scenes from the cult film "Amélie" were shot at the **Café des 2 Moulins** at no. 15. Pop into the tiny, old-fashioned bakery across the street at no. 26, ❷ **INSIDER TIP Les Petits Mitrons**, whose window display is full of tasty looking tarts. Take in the village-like atmosphere **as you continue along rue Abesses, rue Durantin and up rue Tholozé. When you come to the top of rue Lépic,** enjoy the breathtaking view of the golden dome of Les Invalides → p. 30, which shines above the sea of houses.

The garden of the Moulin de la Galette now lies at your feet. The grounds between the two mills, which can still be toured from the outside, were converted into a popular dance hall in the 19th century. Thanks to Auguste Renoir's Impressionist painting of the same name, these gardens are famous around the world. They are now home to the restaurant ❸ **Le Moulin de la Galette** *(dai-*

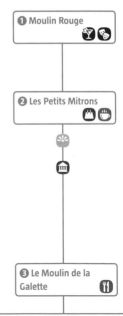

❶ Moulin Rouge

❷ Les Petits Mitrons

❸ Le Moulin de la Galette

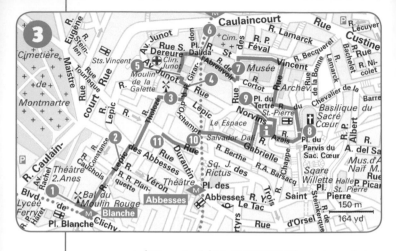

ly | 83, rue Lepic | tel. 01 46 06 84 77 | www.lemoulinde
lagalette.fr | *Moderate*), which is a great place to take
your first break.

④ Place Marcel Aymé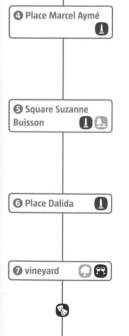

Afterwards, head to **④ Place Marcel Aymé**. Look out for
the quizzical bronze figure emerging from a wall. The
statue depicts the main character of the novella *Le Passe-
muraille (The Man Who Walked through Walls)* and is
a tribute to the writer Marcel Aymé who once lived on
this square. **Follow Avenue Junot and then turn right at
the end of rue Simon Dereure** to get to the little park at
⑤ Square Suzanne Buisson. Sit down and stretch out
your legs on one of the benches and admire the **Statue
of Saint Denis**. St Denis is said to have walked the same
route that you have been following up to now with his
head in his hands.

⑤ Square Suzanne Buisson

⑥ Place Dalida

**Return to the entrance gate and then go up the steps to
the right along a small idyllic path** to **⑥ Place Dalida**.
The statue of the Egyptian-Italian singer (1933–87) looks
up rue de l'Abreuvoir, which winds up the hill lined by
small, crooked houses in a picture-perfect setting. **At the
end of the street and down to the left on rue des Saules**,
there is a surprising little **⑦ vineyard**. The grape harvest in October is celebrated with a festival every year,
the Fête des Vendanges → p. 121. A few yards further
below, the famous cabaret **Au Lapin Agile** ("the agile
rabbit") was once owned by the *chanson* singer Aristide

⑦ vineyard

Bruant who supported many then poor and unknown musicians at the time.

Rue Saint-Vincent will bring you closer to the back side of the gleaming white, almost Byzantine style basilica of ❽ **Sacré-Cœur** → p. 57. Enjoy the view of Paris from the steps on the front side of the church. The narrow lanes around the church filled with souvenir shops and especially the ❾ **Place du Tertre** → p. 57 are always full of tourists and many rather pushy portrait artists who will try to convince you to have your portrait drawn.

Walk down Rue Norvins until you come to rue Gabrielle (Pablo Picasso had his first studio in no. 49), **and then take rue Ravignan to the tree-lined Place Émile Goudeau.** In a studio within the house named ❿ **Bateau-Lavoir**, Picasso's famous cubist painting *Les Demoiselles d'Avignon* came to life. A bit further down, several lovely restaurants will tempt you to end this tour with a good meal. After that, pop into the bar ⓫ **L'atelier Montmartre** (*daily | rue Burq 6 | 18th arr. | tel. 0142513227 | Budget*) – contemporary artists show their work here, and with a little luck, a happening will take place while you're there.

❽ Sacré-Cœur

❾ Place du Tertre

❿ Bateau-Lavoir

⓫ L'atelier Montmartre

With street cafés and portrait painters, Place du Tertre has an almost provincial flair

THE ISLANDS ON THE SEINE AND MARAIS

START: ❶ Musée de Cluny END: ⓮ Musée Picasso	6 hours Walking time (without stops) 1 hour
Distance: ➡ 4 km/2.5 miles	

COSTS: admission to Musée Picasso: 11 euros

IMPORTANT TIPS: the nearest Métro station to the start of the tour on Place Paul Painlevé is M 10 Cluny-La Sorbonne
The nearest Métro station to the last stop on the tour on rue de Thorigny is M8 Chemin Vert

The islands Île de la Cité and Île Saint-Louis are the heart of the metropolis, especially given that the first seeds of the city were sown upon them. The Marais district shines with the glory of the aristocratic palaces *(hôtel particulier)* that were build around the royal square, Place des Vosges, at the beginning of the 17th century. Many Parisians say that this Renaissance-style square in this quite stylish part of town is the most beautiful in the whole city.

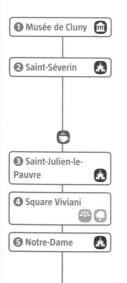

The small park in the shadows of the Roman spas around the ❶ **Musée de Cluny** → p. 50 is the perfect place to start off on the day's tour. A labyrinth of medieval streets begins **on the other side of Boulevard Saint-Germain** around the flamboyant Gothic-style church of ❷ **Saint-Séverin**. The distinguishing features of the church include its five-aisled nave and the double row of columns around the apse. The ribbed vaulted ceiling resembles plant stalks with colourful modern glass windows peeking through. The neighbourhood is full of inviting little cafés such as **La Fourmi Ailée** → p. 68, where you'll be tempted to linger, but also many restaurants that vie for tourist business. **Just a short walk down rue Saint-Séverin** will bring you to the small, stocky church of ❸ **Saint-Julien-le-Pauvre**, the oldest church in the city dating back to the 12th century. From the adjacent park at ❹ **Square Viviani**, you can enjoy the view of the Seine as well as the boxes of Les Bouquinistes → p. 74 and ❺ **Notre Dame Cathedral** → p. 51 in peace and quiet. You simply must go inside the cathedral! A lovely garden brings life to the

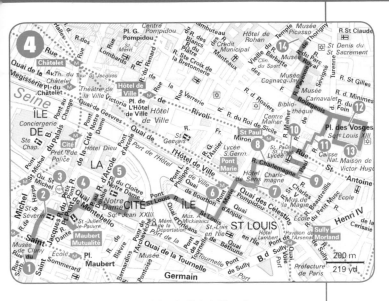

eastern side of the church. Look for the **little bridge that connects the Île de la Cité → p. 48** with the **Île Saint-Louis**. Both islands, as the oldest parts of the city, are the real heart of Paris. Street artists almost always ply their trade on the strip connecting the two. Take some time to window shop on rue Saint-Louis-en-l'Île with its lovely little shops and the best ice cream in the city at ❻ **Amorino** *(daily noon–midnight, closed Dec–Feb | 47, rue Saint-Louis-en-l'Île)*.

The Pont Marie bridge will lead you directly into the Marais quarter. Directly to the right, at the corner of rue de l'Hôtel de Ville and rue du Figuier, the fortress-like late Gothic ❼ **Hôtel de Sens** will surely catch your eye. This former second residence of the powerful bishops of the city of Sens now houses the art library INSIDER TIP **Bibliothèque Forney** which regularly houses exhibitions (equipent.paris.fr/bibliotheque-forney-18). **At the end of rue du Figuier, you will stumble upon rue Charlemagne** and the charming little patio restaurant ❽ **Chez Mademoiselle** *(daily | rue Charlemagne 16 | 4th arr. | tel. 01 42 72 14 16 | Budget–Moderate)*. After a bite to eat, **continue along rue Charlemagne,** past the ruins of a tower and the old city walls dating back to the 13th century. Spend some time browsing through the courtyard laby-

❻ Amorino

❼ Hôtel de Sens

❽ Chez Mademoiselle

rinth of ⑨ **Village Saint-Paul** → p. 74, which is home to approx. 60 antiques dealers selling furniture, artworks, tableware, lamps and jewellery.

Continue left up rue Saint-Paul to the Passage Saint-Paul, which leads through a side entrance into the three-storey Baroque church of ⑩ **Saint-Paul** with its large cupola. The traffic buzzes on rue Saint-Antoine in front of the main entrance. **Walk a bit further towards the Bastille and turn left on rue Caron** to get to the romantic ⑪ **Place du Marché Sainte-Cathérine** → p. 48 with its sycamore trees and cafés. Take a moment to catch your breath before **heading over rue de Turenne to the right onto the lively rue des Francs-Bourgeois,** which is lined by lovely aristocratic palaces. From here, it is just a short walk to the noble ⑫ **Place des Vosges** → p. 48, one of the loveliest squares in the city. Take a walk around it, and, if you want, have a look at the former flat (marked by the flag on the southeastern corner of the square) of the French national poet at ⑬ **Maison Victor Hugo** → p. 47. **Cross back over the square to rue des Francs-Bourgeois, go right on rue Payenne and go via rue du Parc Royal to turn down rue de Thorigny.** The most extensive Picasso collection in the world awaits at the ⑭ **Musée Picasso** → p. 47 in Hôtel Salé. End the day in style at the **Café sur le toit** (Tue–Fri 10.30am–6pm, Sat/Sun 9.30am–6pm | tel. 0144617919 | Budget).

Victor Hugo began work on his masterpiece *Les Misérables* in this room

5

A WALK OF A DIFFERENT KIND BEHIND THE BASTILLE

START: ❶ Métro station Bastille
END: ⓮ Jardin de Reuilly

Distance:
➡ 6.2 km / 3.8 miles

5 hours
walking time
(without stops)
1.5 hours

IMPORTANT TIPS: the M 1, 5 and 8 stop at Bastille; to return to the city centre or the restaurant Pachamama, take the M 8 from Montgallet to Bastille. The Viaduc des Arts is open on Sundays.

In the 19th century, craftsmen ruled over the eastern part of the city behind the Bastille. Nowadays, many of the former workshops *(cours)* have been turned into nostalgic, modern lofts popular among the young and creative crowd. The old train tracks (4.5 km/2.8 miles) running from the east have been transformed into a walking path, and artisans have set up shop in the old aqueduct.

The ❶ **Métro station Bastille** marks the starting point for this tour to the east of the city centre. Nothing remains of the Bastille, the state prison that was stormed in 1789 at the outbreak of the French Revolution. Today, the outline of the former structure is traced in stones different from the rest of the pavement on Place de la Bastille where it intersects with Boulevard Henri IV. Go directly to the shining silver Opéra Bastille → p. 47 and leave this huge, traffic-filled square in the **direction of rue du Faubourg Saint-Antoine.** If you keep a lookout for hidden entrances, you will stumble upon some of the old craftsmen's workshops: **Right at the start of rue de la Roquette** (no. 2), you will come upon the quiet ❷ **Passage du Cheval Blanc**, which is divided into courtyards named after the first six months of the year. **Turn right onto Cité Parchappe to return to rue du Faubourg Saint-Antoine,** which is lined by a string of idyllic courtyards, such as the **Cour Saint-Louis** or the **Cour Vigues**.

At no. 46, at the restaurant ❸ **Pachamama**, where you should make reservations for the evening, you'll see architecture by Gustave Eiffel and South American flair. **Opposite, turn left onto rue de Charonne,** a lively shopping street. At no. 41, treat yourself to a *café crème* on the patio of the trendy ❹ **Pause Café** → p. 69. After-

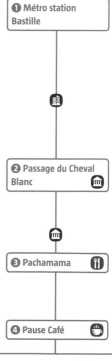

❶ Métro station Bastille

❷ Passage du Cheval Blanc

❸ Pachamama

❹ Pause Café

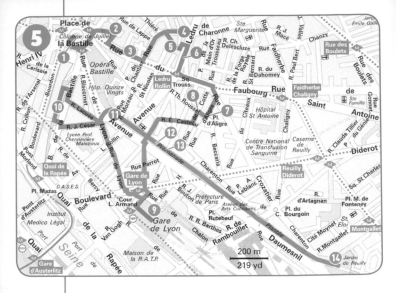

⑤ Passage Lhomme 🏛

⑥ Chocolaterie Pause Détente 🛍

⑦ Marché d'Aligre 🛍

⑧ Le Baron Rouge 🍴

⑨ Gare de Lyon 🏛

⑩ Bassin de l'Arsenal ⚓

⑪ Promenade Plantée 🚶🏛

wards, cross through the lushly landscaped, picturesque **⑤ Passage Lhomme until it emerges onto Avenue Ledru-Rollin.** Stop at no. 98 and select some chocolates from **⑥ Chocolaterie Pause Détente** *(closed Mon)* to eat as you walk on. **Back on rue Faubourg Saint-Antoine, turn right into rue Crozatier until you reach rue d'Aligre, which will take you directly to Place d'Aligre.** At the 200-year old, still very authentic market hall of **⑦ INSIDERTIP Marché d'Aligre → p. 77** you will find no end of delicious cheeses, hams, sausages and cold cuts. A good glass of wine and a few oysters at **⑧ Le Baron Rouge → p. 71** are just right for a little break.

With this fine taste lingering in your mouth, **follow rue Emilio Castelar and then rue Traversière to get to ⑨ Gare de Lyon**, the loveliest railway station in the city and home to the legendary restaurant **Le Train Bleu → p. 65**. Then take **rue de Lyon and rue Jules César** to the picture-perfect harbour **⑩ Bassin de l'Arsenal**. The port has an almost maritime flair thanks to the many yachts that lay anchor here. **Go back via rue Lacuée to Avenue Daumnesnil,** which will bring you to this tour's major highlight: the **⑪ Promenade Plantée** (aka: Coulée Verte).

These former train tracks now surrounded by plenty of vegetation lead 4.5 km (2.8 miles) from the Bastille to the forest of Vincennes.

⑫ Viaduc des Arts 🛍

For the first 1.5 km (1 mile), the red brick arches of the former railway viaduct have been glassed in to create studio space for all kinds of artisans and craftsmen. Whilst products are made and sold in the shops below, you can walk along the planted roof. **There are plenty of stairs that will take you up the 9 m (30 ft) to the top.** In the more than 50 studio shops within the ⑫ **Viaduc des Arts** → p. 81, only the finest materials are used. Fashion designers, goldsmiths, picture restorers, glass-blowers and many shops selling art as opposed to crafts are housed in this innovative space. For something a bit different, check out the jewellery designer **Tzuri Gueta** (no. 1) who, among other things, creates silicon objects that resemble underwater plants. Interesting jewellery is also created at **Cécile et Jeanne** (no. 49) If you have deeper pockets, you can buy your own unique made-to-order handbag at **Serge Amoruso** (no. 37) or have an umbrella designed and made just for you at **Heurtault** (no. 85). If all this shopping has made you hungry, the best and most convenient place to go is the ⑬ **Viaduc Café** (daily | no. 41–43 | tel. 01 44 74 70 70 | www. leviaduc-cafe.com | Budget).

⑬ Viaduc Café 🍴

⑭ Jardin de Reuilly 🌳

Ateliers and shops beneath the old vaults of the Viaduc des Arts

Once you're duly refreshed, climb up to the "roof" of the viaduct and admire the urban walking trail. Between the rose bushes, lavender and babbling water, you can appreciate the extraordinary view of the surrounding metropolitan area. **As you continue to the east**, you will come to the small park ⑭ **Jardin de Reuilly**, which is spanned by a footbridge and a favourite place among the locals in the neighbourhood during the summer. Take time to relax for a bit in the park before you head back.

TRAVEL WITH KIDS

AQUABOULEVARD (156 B5) (*ₘ D12*)
One of the largest water parks in Europe, featuring pools with waterfalls and a number of fun waterslides under its glass roof. *Mon–Thu 9am–11pm, Fri 9am–midnight, Sat 8am–midnight | admission 29–33 euros, children 3–11 yr. 19 euros | 4, rue Louis Armand | 15th arr. | M 8 Balard | www.aquaboulevard.com*

CANAL SAINT-MARTIN
Nice, almost three-hour canal trip between the Musée d'Orsay (146 A4) (*ₘ J7*) and the Parc de la Villette (143 E2) (*ₘ Q2*) through locks, bridges and tunnels. *Mar–Nov daily | departure: 9.45am from the Quai Anatole France or 2.30pm from Parc de la Villette | 20 euros, children 4–11 y. 13 euros, 12–25 y. 17 euros | tel. 01 42 40 96 97 | www.pariscanal.com*

CIRQUE D'HIVER (148 B4) (*ₘ O7*)
The more than 150 years old circus venue is regarded as one of the most beautiful in the world. The Bouglione family provides the best in circus tradition from Sept to March. *Fri 8.30pm, Sat/Sun, sometimes Wed 10.45am, 2pm, 5.15pm, 8.30pm | admission 12–62 euros on the internet | 110, rue Amelot | 11th arr. | M 8 Filles du Calvaire | www.cirquedhiver.com*

CITÉ DES SCIENCES ET DE L'INDUSTRIE ★ (143 E2) (*ₘ Q1–2*)
A futuristic science museum where visitors can pretend to be researchers with a submarine, flight simulator and planetarium. The giant silver ball *La Géode* provides a 360-degree big screen presentation on scientific topics every hour. *Tue–Sat 10am–6pm, Sun 10am–7pm | prices structured according to selection of attractions starting at 12 euros; children 9 euros | 30, av. Cortenin Cariiou | 19th arr. | M 7 Porte de la Villette | www.cite-sciences.fr*

DISNEYLAND PARIS (0) (*ₘ 0*)
12 million visitors every year make Walt Disney's fairy-tale dreamland Europe's most important tourist attraction. *Daily, opening hours on the website | day pass from 75 euros, children from 67 euros | cheaper offers on the internet | 40 km (25 miles) east of Paris | RER A Marne-de-la Vallée – Chessy | www.disneylandparis.fr*

JARDIN D'ACCLIMATATION (136–137 B–E6) (*ₘ B4–5*)
In this elegant area in the Bois de Boulogne, this garden exudes the charm of the 19th century with its unusual playground areas, carousels, animals and

Fun for kids of all ages:
Sure, Paris has something in store
for toddlers as well as for teens

water features. *Mon–Fri 10am–6pm, Sat/Sun 10am–7pm | admission 3 euros, children under 3 free | M 1 Les Sablons | www.jardindacclimatation.fr*

JARDIN DES PLANTES
(153 F2–3) (*N10*)
Something for every age group: at the Jardin des Plantes with its free *horticultural teaching garden (daily 7.30am–7pm)* there is also the INSIDER TIP *Ménagerie (daily 9am–5/6.30pm depending on the season | admission 13 euros, children 9 euros, free under 4 yr.)*, a zoo for smaller children with reptiles, monkeys and wildcats. On the side of the park opposite the zoo, older children can explore the ★ *Muséum National d'Histoire Naturelle (daily 10am–6pm | admission from 9 euros, free under 26 yr.)*. In the entrance hall there is a fascinating caravan of stuffed life-size animals. You can also check out the complexes for *palaeontology* (with huge dinosaur bones) and *mineralogy (daily 10am–5/6pm | admission 6/7 euros,* *free/reduced under 26 yr.)*. The ● greenhouses, *Les Grandes Serres (summer: daily 10am–6pm, winter: daily 10am–5pm | admission 7 euros, children 5 euros (free under 4 yr.)*, with their rain forest vegetation are also fantastic. *5th arr. | M 5, 10, RER C Gare d'Austerlitz | www.mnhn.fr | www.jardindesplantes.net | www.zoodu jardindesplantes.fr*

PARC ASTÉRIX (0) (*0*)
A good French alternative to Disneyland, a bit smaller. Asterix and his friends captivate visitors with all sorts of fun rides and a replica of the small village of the indomitable Gauls. *April–Nov daily 10am–6pm, sometimes 10pm (outside of the school holidays partly closed during the week) | admission 47 euros, children (3–11 yr.) 39 euros, early-bird tariffs on the internet | 60128-Plailly (30 km/18½ miles north of Paris) | by bus: from the Louvre coach park (M 1, 7 Palais Royal-Louvre) departure: 9am (23 euros) | by car: motorway A 1, exit: Parc Astérix | www.parcasterix.fr*

FESTIVALS & EVENTS

EVENTS

FEBRUARY

Chinese New Year: colourful procession around the Place d'Italie (dates vary)

MARCH–APRIL

Foire de Catou: large and interesting antique trade fair (additional dates in September and October). *RER A Chatou-Croissy*

Banlieues Bleues: first-rate jazz festival in Saint-Denis and other suburbs. *www.banlieuesbleues.org*

MAY

Nuit européenne des musées: Many Paris museums take part in the annual European night of the museums

MAY–JUNE

Festival de Saint-Denis: the classical music festival starts at the end of May and continues for four weeks. *www.festival-saint-denis.fr*

French Open: Around 60 000 tennis balls get played each year, when the best players meet each other in the Stade Roland-Garros. *www.rolandgarros.com*

JUNE

Dîner en Blanc: flashmob-like mass picnic with thousands of participants

★ *Fête de la Musique:* free concerts on nearly every street corner in the city all night long (21/22 June).

Marche des fiertés lesbiennes, gaies, bi et trans: gay, lesbian, bi and trans procession through the centre (fourth Saturday)

JUNE–JULY

INSIDER TIP *Paris Jazz Festival:* free concerts with international jazz greats in the Parc Floral des Bois de Vincennes every weekend. *www.parisjazzfestival.fr*

JULY

Bastille Day: large military parade on the Champs-Elysées and fireworks on the Place du Trocadéro, in the evening and the night before INSIDER TIP balls in the fire brigade's barracks (14 July)

Tour de France: final stage on the Champs-Elysées (last or second to last Sunday)

JULY–AUGUST

● INSIDER TIP *Paris-Plages:* various beach activities for five weeks beginning in mid-July

The metropolis offers something for everyone: music, theatre, cinema, sport, cultural events and colourful parades

Quartier d'Eté (www.quartierdete.com): many free concerts in parks and on small squares (from mid-July)

Open-air Cinema: free cinema at Parc de la Villette (from mid-July)

AUGUST

Rock en Seine: well-known rock music greats perform for three days in the Parc de Saint-Cloud. *www.rockenseine.com*

SEPTEMBER

Journées européennes du patrimoine: free admission to public buildings otherwise closed to the general public (third weekend)

SEPTEMBER–DECEMBER

★ *Festival d'Automne:* autumn festival with theatre, music and dance performances. *www.festival-automne.com*

OCTOBER

Fête des Vendanges (www.fetedesvendangesdemontmartre.com): party to celebrate the grape harvest on Montmartre (first Saturday)

Fiac: extensive contemporary art fair

INSIDER TIP *Nuit Blanche:* music and art happenings all night long, partly in unusual places (usually on the first Saturday)

NATIONAL HOLIDAYS

1 Jan	New Year's Day
22 April 2019, 13 April 2020	
	Easter Monday
1 May	Labour Day
8 May	Victory Day
10 June 2019, 21 May 2020	
	Ascension Day
14 July	Bastille Day
15 Aug	Assumption of Mary
1 Nov	All Saints' Day
11 Nov	Armistice Day
25 Dec	Christmas

LINKS, BLOGS, APPS & MORE

LINKS & BLOGS

www.quefaire.paris A shared calendar managed by the city of Paris; private individuals as well as club and event location managers can announce events here

www.paris-26-gigapixels.com Inspiring interactive page which uses the Google Earth principle to navigate through Paris and to simultaneously obtain information about the most important attractions

www.mylittleparis.com Lifestyle tips – restaurants, beauty & fashion, special sales and more

www.myparisianlife.com Stylish blog by a New York expat – eating, drinking, shopping, beauty, activities with kids and much more, sorted by arrondissement, if you want

www.google.com/maps/d/viewer?mid=13LegxAI4GtfeUzV6fb4u_goTOGA&hl=fr&ll=48.8593362498122%2C2.322599500000024&z=13 Interactive map for locating and downloading literary classics with references to Paris

www.spottedbylocals.com/paris Parisians and newcomers post articles here about their favourite spots in the city – cool and casual. Also available as an app for a few euros

www.cityguide-index.com As a single traveller, you can use this portal to contact local guides in the city

VIDEOS

www.youtube.com/watch?v=NY5Xtc6YuCg&feature=youtu.be The song "Titi Parisien" is an homage to Paris. It was recorded after the terrorist attacks of 13 November 2015 by French rappers Seth Gueko, Nekfeu and Oxmo Puccino

www.youtube.com/watch?v=yV2HSvdwEI To help boost tourism in the wake of the terrorist attacks, the city

Regardless of whether you are still researching your trip or already in Paris: these addresses will provide you with more information, videos and networks to make your holiday even more enjoyable

of Paris published a declaration of love to itself in September 2016 with the video "Paris, je t'aime"

www.youtube.com/watch?v=e_M807HAe2c&feature=youtu.be Two Parisian artists felt that the glossy video clip mentioned above didn't reflect their own aesthetic and attitude, so they published a response: "Paris, on t'aime aussi" ("Paris, we love you too"), which features real Parisians, not actors. The film provides a glimpse behind the city's glittering facade

www.3motspour.paris "3 Words for Paris": an interactive website that lets you create your own Paris video by entering three words that you associate with the city. The page is available in French and English

Citymapper Car, bicycle, Métro, bus, train, tram or walking? What's the best way to get from A to B? This app has the answer!

LittleBigCity Interactive event app that does more than just tell you what's going on in your immediate surroundings; it also provides you with discount tickets and lets you communicate with other users

Où faire pipi à Paris This app lets you know where you can stop to relieve yourself when you're on the go: 200 freely accessible toilets in administrative buildings, hospitals, libraries and businesses that you would never find on your own

SAIP – Système d'alerte et d'information des populations After the most recent series of terrorist attacks, the French interior ministry developed this app to warn the public in case a future attack occurs

Fudo This app shows you restaurants near your location where you can still find a free table for the number of people you're with; it also reserves the table for you and pays the bill when you're done

Welcome to Paris With this new free app from the Paris tourist information agency, you have everything you need for your trip right in your pocket

TRAVEL TIPS

ARRIVAL

Driving in Paris is no fun at all: loads of traffic, expensive car parks that are always full, an eternal search for a free spot, wheel clamps and tow trucks for parking offenders. Can't do without a car? Then make sure your accommodation offers parking, or reserve a space in a car park *(www.parkingsdeparis.com/EN)*.

The motorways are toll-based with a speed limit of 130 km/h/80mph, and they all lead to the chaotic ring road Boulevard Périphérique (Périph for short) with 38 "portes" where you can enter and exit.

Keep in mind: A vignette has been required for nearly all vehicles in Paris since 2017. This emissions sticker is available in six different versions. On weekdays from 8am to 8pm, vehicles with high emissions are not permitted on the roads. The sticker must be placed in a visible location on the inside of the vehicle's windscreen, or the driver will face a fine of 68 euros. The sticker costs 4.80 euros. It can be ordered online from the French environmental ministry's website: *www.certificat-air.gouv.fr*.

You can travel between London and Paris by coach for as little as £ 12 one way. Check out the National Express connections between London and Paris at www.nationalexpress.com.

The TGV, the Thalys and the Eurostar (from London) arrive at the Gare du Nord. The railway station has a connection to the Métro network and the RER B can also be accessed from the Gare du Nord. Tickets can be bought on the restaurant coaches of the trains. If you book early enough, you can travel from London to Paris return from 88 euros.

Due to stiff competition, you can often get a cheap flight to Paris by booking in advance, and even bargains can be found at short notice. Return flights are often available through *Easyjet* from 99 euros. Compare airfares on the Internet under *www.skyscanner.net*. Scheduled flights out of the UK land either at *Roissy-Charles-de-Gaulle (CDG)* airport north of Paris, or at *Orly (ORY)* to the south of the city.

You can get to and from the airport with public transport provided by RATP *(www.ratp.fr)*:

It's fast and reliable, as long as there isn't a strike or an accident slowing things down. The suburban train line

RESPONSIBLE TRAVEL

It doesn't take a lot to be environmentally friendly whilst travelling. Don't just think about your carbon footprint whilst flying to and from your holiday destination but also about how you can protect nature and culture abroad. As a tourist it is especially important to respect nature, look out for local products, cycle instead of driving, save water and much more. If you would like to find out more about eco-tourism please visit: *www.ecotourism.org*

From arrival to weather

RER B travels from CDG via Paris to Antony every few minutes; from Antony, the Orlyval light railway runs to Orly Airport. *CDG–Paris: Runs from shortly before 5am until just before midnight | travel time: 25–30 min. | 10 euros. ORY–Paris: 6am–11pm| travel time: 40 min. | 12.05 euros (RER plus Orlyval).*

The Roissy and Orly buses travel directly to Paris; the trip can take quite a bit longer if there's trafic. *CDG–Opéra: 6am.–12.30 am (runs from 5.15am in the opposite direction) every 15–20 min. | travel time: 60–75 min. | 11.50 euros. ORY–RER and Métro station Denfert-Rochereau: 6am–12.30 am (runs from 5.35 am–midnight in the opposite direction) every 8–15 min.| travel time: approx. 30 min. | 8 euros.*

The bus lines 350 (Gare de l'Est) and 351 (Nation) also run from Paris to CDG Airport, as do the night bus lines N140 and N143. Bus line 183 (Porte de Choisy), tram line 7 and night buses N22, N31, N131 and N144 run to ORY. They're a bit cheaper, but they take longer because they make numerous stops.

The sleek new airport buses from *Le bus direct (www.lebusdirect.com)* are equipped with WiFi and USB ports. *CDG: 17 euros, ORY: 12 euros.* Taxi: A ride downtown costs 50–55 euros from CDG and 30–35 euros from ORY.

BIKE RENTALS

If you want to explore Paris by bicycle, take a *Vélib' (www.velibmetropole. fr)*. The entire fleet of bicycles is being upgraded in 2018. Now, you can also rent e-bikes (in blue) at the company's approximately 1,400 docking stations throughout the city. If you choose one of the green Vélib' models, though, you'll have to work the pedals yourself. For a day ticket, you'll pay a base price of 5 euros; a whole week costs 15 euros. The first half hour on a normal bicycle is free; each half hour after that costs

BUDGETING

Coffee	£ 0.90/$ 1.17– £ 7.25/$ 9.33 for an espresso
Snack	£ 2.26/$ 2.90–£ 5.43/$ 7 for a ham sandwich
Wine	£ 4/$ 5.25–£ 18/$ 23 for a glass of table wine
Métro	£ 1.36/$ 1.75 for a single ticket
Souvenir	£ 15.45/$ 19.95 for 6 macarons from Ladurée
Taxi	£ 7.70/$ 9.90 for a short trip of approx. 4 km/2.5 miles

1 euro. For an e-bike, the first half hour costs 1 euro, and each half hour after that costs 2 euros. You'll find a Vélib' station every 300 metres or so. By the way: If the seat of a parked bicycle is turned backwards, it means that the last rider discovered the bicycle doesn't work properly. The Vélib' app is really practical: It shows you where the closest station is located and how many bicycles are currently available there.

There are little signs on many traffic lights to indicate to cyclists that they can turn right or keep going straight when the light turns red.

CUSTOMS

Within the European Union the following quality and quantity limits apply for personal consumption: 800 cigarettes, 1 kg tobacco, 10 l spirits. For wine there's no benchmark.

EMBASSIES & CONSULATES

BRITISH EMBASSY
35, rue du Faubourg St Honoré | 75383 Paris Cedex 08 | tel. 01 44 51 31 00 | www. gov.uk/government/world/france

EMBASSY OF THE UNITED STATES
2, avenue Gabriel | 75008 Paris Cedex 08 | tel. 01 43 12 22 22 | www.usembassy. gov/france

EMBASSY OF CANADA
130, rue du Faubourg St Honoré | 75008 Paris | tel. 01 44 43 29 00 | www.cana dainternational.gc.ca/france/offices-bureaux/contact.aspx?lang=eng

EMERGENCY SERVICES

– Ambulance (Samu): dial 15
– Police: dial 17
– Fire department, First Aid: dial 18
– Medical emergencies (SOS Médecins): tel. 01 47 07 77 77
– Dental emergencies: tel. 01 43 37 51 00

GUIDED TOURS

Of course, Paris has sightseeing buses: *www.bigbustours.com/paris* or *www. paris.opentour.com*, but that's not all:

PARIS À VÉLO
Paris wants to become the bicycle capital by 2020. Growing numbers of tour guides are also using the new infrastructure. Many English tours are available from companies like *Paris Bike Tour (from 34 euros | 13, rue Brantôme | 3rd arr. | M 11 Rambuteau | tel. 01 42 74 22 14 | www. parisbiketour.net)*

ON FOUR WHEELS UNDER AN UMBRELLA
A classic: Travel from tourist attraction to tourist attraction in a Citroën 2CV. The chauffeurs from *4 roues sous 1 parapluie (tours from 20 euros/person | tel. 01 58 59 27 82 | www.4roues-sous-1para pluie.com)*do more than just rattle off a prepared script – they have loads of tips up their sleeves.

INFORMATION BEFORE YOU TRAVEL

On the page of the French tourism office *Atout France (www.france.fr)* you'll find a lot of helpful information, and on the website of the *Office du Tourisme et des Congrès de Paris (www.parisinfo.com)* you can book accomodation and activities.

INFORMATION IN PARIS

Info points of the tourist information:
Main office: *25, rue des Pyramides | 1st arr. | M 7, 14 Pyramides | RER A Auber | May–Oct daily 9am–7pm, Nov–April 10am–7pm*
Paris Rendez-vous (25, rue de Rivoli | 4th arr. | M 1, 11 Hôtel de Ville | Mon–Sat 10.30am–6.30pm)
Gare du Nord (18, rue de Dunkerque | 10th arr. | M 4, 5 Gare du Nord | RER B, D Gare du Nord | daily 8am–6pm)

Gare de l'Est (pl. du 11 novembre 1918 | 10th arr. | M 4, 5, 7 Gare de l'Est | Mon–Sat 8am–7pm)

Montmartre (blvd. Rochechouart | opposite no. 72 | 18th arr. | M 2 Anvers | daily 10am–6pm)

INTERNET & WIFI

Around 400 public squares, parks and buildings such as libraries and the Centre Pompidou offer free WiFi. Signs denote places with WiFi. The service is usually accessible from 7am to 11pm. An increasing number of cafés, bars, restaurants as well as hotels and youth hostels provide *wifi gratuit.* Some Métro and RER stations are equipped with Internet stations with free access.

LOST & FOUND

BUREAU DES OBJETS TROUVÉS
36, rue des Morillons | 15th arr. | tel. 08 21 00 25 25 (*) | M 12 Convention | Mon–Thu 8.30am–5pm, Fri 8.30am–4.30pm

MEDICAL SERVICES

EU citizens are entitled to the same health benefits as the French by means of the European Health Insurance Card (EHIC). You can also offset physician expenses through the French social insurance provider, although a full refund is not typically issued. Travel insurance is recommended – also for US citizens. Chemists *(pharmacies)* are denoted by a green cross and are generally open until 8pm Mon–Sat, or even later. Pharmacies open at night and on the weekend can be found at *www.mono pharmacien-idf.fr*.

PHONES & MOBILE PHONES

All Paris numbers (with the exception of special numbers beginning with 09) begin with 01. Mobile numbers start with 06 or 07, if they are newer numbers, special numbers with 08. The country code for the UK is +44, for the USA +1, and then the area code without a zero. When calling from overseas, +33 must be dialled for Paris phone numbers (leaving out the zero).

The French word for mobile phone is *portable*. By the way, you can INSIDER TIP charge your mobile at the new bus stops in Paris with a USB cable.

POST

The historic main office *(52, rue du Louvre | 1st arr. | M 4 Les Halles | ww.laposte.fr)* is closed until the end of 2018 due to renovations. Until then: *16, rue Étienne Marcel | 2nd arr. | M 4 Étienne Marcel | daily 7.30am–6am*. Cost of sending postcards and letters up to 20 grams within the EU is 1 euro.

PUBLIC TRANSPORT

If you're in a hurry, it's best to take the Métro or the underground urban area RER railway. If you're changing trains and carry heavy luggage, note that many stations have long passageways and flights of stairs.

If you have time and want to see something of the city, buses and trams are perfect. This is especially the case for bus number 73 (Arc de Triomphe, Champs-Elysées, Place de la Concorde, Musée d'Orsay) and number 21 (Opéra Garnier, Palais Royal, Louvre, Île de la Cité, St-Michel, Jardin du Luxembourg, Rue Mouffetard). This way, a INSIDER TIP city tour by bus will only cost you 1.90 euros!

Métro and RER operate from 5.30am–1am, Fri, Sat and before holidays an hour longer. Buses, depending on the line, start later in the morning and stop their service earlier in the evening. Night buses *(noctilien)* run between 12.30am and 5.30am. Timetables for all Métro, RER, tram and bus lines are available at all stations and at *www.ratp.fr* or the RATP app.

Single tickets *ticket t+* are valid within the city limits for the Métro, RER, tram and buses. They are valid for two hours on the Métro and RER, with as many transfers as you wish. Buses and trams can be used for 1.5 hours, also with as many transfers as you wish. Be aware that changing from Métro/RER to a bus or tram will cost you a further single ticket. Tickets can be purchased at tobacco shops marked with the ticket pictogram, in all Métro and RER stations as well as from bus drivers (10 cents surcharge). A single ticket costs 1.90 euros (a night bus can cost 1–5 single tickets, depending on the distance). It is more economical to purchase a book of 10 tickets *(carnet)* for 14.50 euros. Children up to four years of age travel for free, with a special rate for children between four and ten.

The day card *Carte Mobilis* costs 7.30 euros. The *Paris Visite* ticket costs 11.65 euros per day for Paris and the adjacent suburbs and 24.50 euros for all zones. It offers additional discounts for several attractions. The *Paris Navigo Decouverte* (22.15 euros/week, 73 euros/month plus 5 euros for the ticket and a passport photo) is ideal for a longer Paris stay. It allows you to travel as often as you wish in all zones on weekdays. You can only purchase these tickets at the beginning of the week/month.

SEINE EXCURSIONS

Numerous tourist boats are waiting to take you past Tour Eiffel, Louvre and

WEATHER IN PARIS

	Jan.	Feb.	March	April	May	June	July	Aug.	Sept.	Oct.	Nov.	Dec.
Daytime temperatures in °C/°F												
	6/43	7/45	12/54	16/61	20/68	23/73	25/77	24/75	21/70	16/61	10/50	7/45
Nighttime temperatures in °C/°F												
	1/34	1/34	4/40	6/43	10/50	13/55	15/59	14/57	12/54	8/46	5/41	2/36
☀ Sunshine hours/day	2	3	5	7	7	7	7	7	6	4	2	2
☂ Precipitation days/month	12	10	8	9	9	9	9	9	9	8	10	10

Notre-Dame. You can choose between sightseeing and restaurant trips. The *bateaux mouches* (*April–Sept 10.15am–10.30pm, Oct–March 11am–9.20pm, every 20 min. | departures: Port de la Conférence, Pont de l'Alma (8th arr.) | M 9 Alma-Marceau | duration: 70 min. | 13.50 euros, incl.lunch 60 euros, incl. dinner 75–155 euros*) are legendary.

Or take a *Batobus (www.batobus.com)*. These ferries stop at nine spots where you can embark and disembark as you please. Frequency and departure times vary depending on the season. *Day ticket 17 euros*.

TAXIS & VTC

Taxis charge a base fee of 2.60 euros and cost between 1.06 and 1.58 euros per km (depending on the time of travel) with a minimum fare of 7 euros. There are additional costs for reservations, waiting times and parties of more than four passengers, but not for luggage. The only fixed prices are for trips to the airport (see p. 125). With the app "Paris Taxi" provided by the city of Pairs, you can order a taxi and rate your trip. You have to pay the driver directly.

– *Taxi G7: 01 47 39 47 39 | tel. www.g7.fr*. App with integrated payment function.

– *Taxis Bleus: tel. 01 49 36 10 10 | www. taxis-bleus.com*. App with integrated payment and minimum price function.

You can book and pay for trips with a V.T.C. *(Voiture de Tourisme avec Chauffeur)* via the corresponding app: *Uber (www.uber. com) | leCab (tel. 01 76 49 76 49 | www. lecab.fr) | Marcel (tel. 01 70 95 14 15 | www.marcel.cab)*: Great deals for early bookers!

TICKET SALES

Either you visit one of the eleven Paris branches of *Fnac*, or you order at *www. fnacspectacles.com*.

Reduced theatre and concert tickets are available at *billetreduc.com*.

WHAT'S ON

L'Officiel du Spectacle (0.70 euros) provide an overview of what's on in Paris. Published every Wednesday, also available as an app *(www.offi.fr)*.

CURRENCY CONVERTER

£	€	€	£
1	1.14	1	0.88
3	3.43	3	2.63
5	5.70	5	4.38
13	14.85	13	11.38
40	46	40	35
75	86	75	66
120	137	120	105
250	286	250	219
500	571	500	438

$	€	€	$
1	0.81	1	1.23
3	2.43	3	3.70
5	4.05	5	6.17
13	10.54	13	16.04
40	32.42	40	49.35
75	61	75	92.52
120	97	120	148
250	203	250	308
500	405	500	617

For current exchange rates see www.xe.com

USEFUL PHRASES FRENCH

IN BRIEF

Yes/No/Maybe	oui/non/peut-être
Please/Thank you	s'il vous plaît/merci
Good morning!/afternoon!/	Bonjour!/Bonjour!/
evening!/night!	Bonsoir!/Bonne nuit!
Hello!/goodbye!/See you!	Salut!/Au revoir!/Salut!
Excuse me, please	Pardon!
My name is...	Je m'appelle...
I'm from...	Je suis de...
May I ...?/ Pardon?	Puis-je ...?/Comment?
I would like to.../	Je voudrais .../
have you got...?	Avez-vous?
How much is...?	Combien coûte...?
I (don't) like this	Ça (ne) me plaît (pas).
good/bad/broken	bon/mauvais/cassé
too much/much/little	trop/beaucoup/peu
all/nothing	tout/rien
Help!/Attention!	Au secours/attention
police/fire brigade/	police/pompiers/
ambulance	ambulance
Could you please help me?	Est-ce que vous pourriez m'aider?
Do you speak English?	Parlez-vous anglais?
Do you understand?	Est-ce que vous comprenez?
Could you please ...?	Pourriez vous ... s'il vous plait?
...repeat that	répéter
...speak more slowly	parler plus lentement
...write that down	l'écrire

DATE & TIME

Monday/Tuesday	lundi/mardi
Wednesday/Thursday	mercredi/jeudi
Friday/Saturday/	vendredi/samedi/
Sunday	dimanche
working day/holiday	jour ouvrable/jour férié
today/tomorrow/	aujourd'hui /demain/
yesterday	hier
hour/minute	heure/minute
day/night/week	jour/nuit/semaine
month/year	mois/année
What time is it?	Quelle heure est-t-il?

Tu parles français?

"Do you speak French?" This guide will help you to say the basic words and phrases in French.

It's three o'clock	Il est trois heures
It's half past three.	Il est trois heures et demi
a quarter to four	quatre heures moins le quart

TRAVEL

open/closed	ouvert/fermé
entrance/exit	entrée/sortie
departure/arrival	départ/arrivée
toilets/restrooms /	toilettes/
ladies/gentlemen	femmes/hommes
(no) drinking water	eau (non) potable
Where is...?/Where are...?	Où est...?/Où sont...?
left/right	à gauche/à droite
straight ahead/back	tout droit/en arrière
close/far	près/loin
bus/tram/underground / taxi/cab	bus/tramway/métro/taxi
stop/cab stand	arrêt/station de taxi
parking lot/parking garage	parking
street map/map	plan de ville/carte routière
train station/harbour/	gare/port/
airport	aéroport
schedule/ticket	horaire/billet
single/return	aller simple/aller-retour
train/track/platform	train/voie/quai
I would like to rent...	Je voudrais... louer.
a car/a bicycle/	une voiture/un vélo/
a boat	un bateau
petrol/gas station	station d'essence
petrol/gas / diesel	essence/diesel
breakdown/repair shop	panne/garage

FOOD & DRINK

The menu, please	La carte, s'il vous plaît.
Could I please have ...?	Puis-je avoir ... s'il vous plaît
bottle/carafe/glass	bouteille/carafe/verre
knife/fork/spoon	couteau/fourchette/cuillère
salt/pepper/sugar	sel/poivre/sucre
vinegar/oil	vinaigre/huile
milk/cream/lemon	lait/crème/citron
cold/too salty/not cooked	froid/trop salé/pas cuit

with/without ice/sparkling	avec/sans glaçons/gaz
vegetarian	végétarien(ne)
May I have the bill, please	Je voudrais payer, s'il vous plaît
bill	addition

SHOPPING

pharmacy/chemist	pharmacie/droguerie
baker/market	boulangerie/marché
shopping centre	centre commercial
department store	grand magasin
100 grammes/1 kilo	cent grammes/un kilo
expensive/cheap/price	cher/bon marché/prix
more/less	plus/moins
organically grown	de l'agriculture biologique

ACCOMMODATION

I have booked a room	J'ai réservé une chambre
Do you have any ... left?	Avez-vous encore ...?
single room/double room	chambre simple/double
breakfast	petit déjeuner
half board/	demi-pension/
full board (American plan)	pension complète
shower/sit-down bath	douche/bain
balcony/terrace	balcon /terrasse
key/room card	clé/carte magnétique
luggage/suitcase/bag	bagages/valise/sac

BANKS, MONEY & CREDIT CARDS

bank/ATM/pin code	banque/guichet automatique/code
cash/credit card	comptant/carte de crédit
bill/coin	billet/monnaie

HEALTH

doctor/dentist/	médecin/dentiste/
paediatrician	pédiatre
hospital/emergency clinic	hôpital/urgences
fever/pain	fièvre/douleurs
diarrhoea/nausea	diarrhée/nausée
sunburn	coup de soleil
inflamed/injured	enflammé/blessé
plaster/bandage	pansement/bandage
ointment/pain reliever	pommade/analgésique

POST, TELECOMMUNICATIONS & MEDIA

stamp	timbre
lettre/postcard	lettre/carte postale
I need a landline phone card	J'ai besoin d'une carte téléphonique pour fixe.
I'm looking for a prepaid card for my mobile	Je cherche une recharge pour mon portable.
Where can I find internet access?	Où puis-je trouver un accès à internet?
dial/connection/engaged	composer/connection/occupé
socket/charger	prise électrique/chargeur
computer/battery/rechargeable battery	ordinateur/batterie/ accumulateur
at sign (@)	arobase
internet address (URL)/ e-mail address	adresse internet/ mail
internet connection/wifi	accès internet/wi-fi
e-mail/file/print	mail/fichier/imprimer

LEISURE, SPORTS & BEACH

beach	plage
sunshade/lounger	parasol/transat
low tide/high tide/current	marée basse/marée haute/courant
cable car/chair lift	téléphérique/télésiège
(rescue) hut	refuge

NUMBERS

0	zéro	17	dix-sept
1	un, une	18	dix-huite
2	deux	19	dix-neuf
3	trois	20	vingt
4	quatre	30	trente
5	cinq	40	quarante
6	six	50	cinquante
7	sept	60	soixante
8	huit	70	soixante-dix
9	neuf	80	quatre-vingt
10	dix	90	quatre-vingt-dix
11	onze	100	cent
12	douze	200	deux cents
13	treize	1000	mille
14	quatorze		
15	quinze	½	un[e] demi[e]
16	seize	¼	un quart

STREET ATLAS

The green line indicates the Discovery Tour "Paris at a glance"
The blue line indicates the other Discovery Tours
All tours are also marked on the pull-out map

Photo: Notre-Dame

Exploring Paris

The map on the back cover shows how the area has been sub-divided

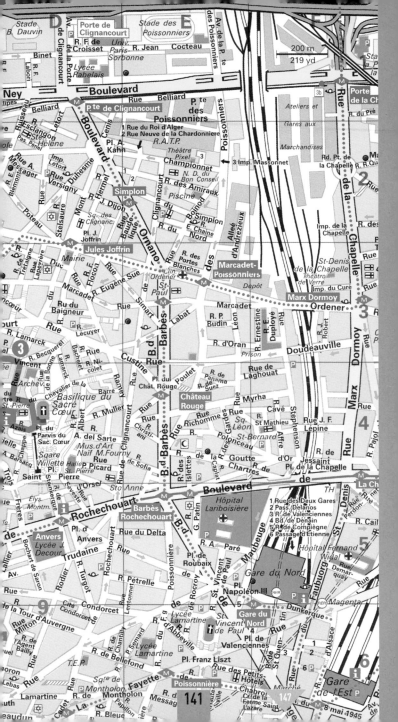

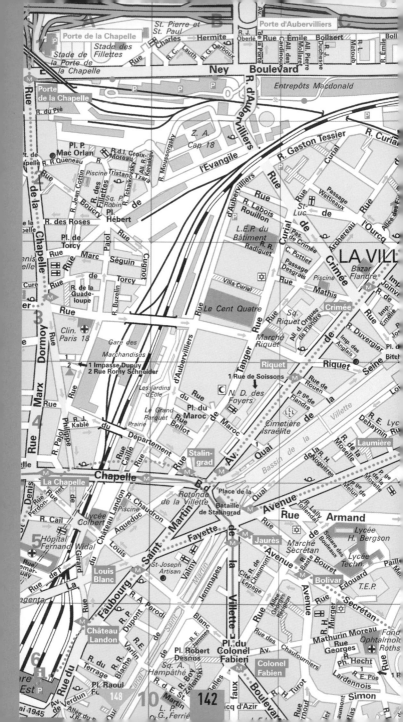

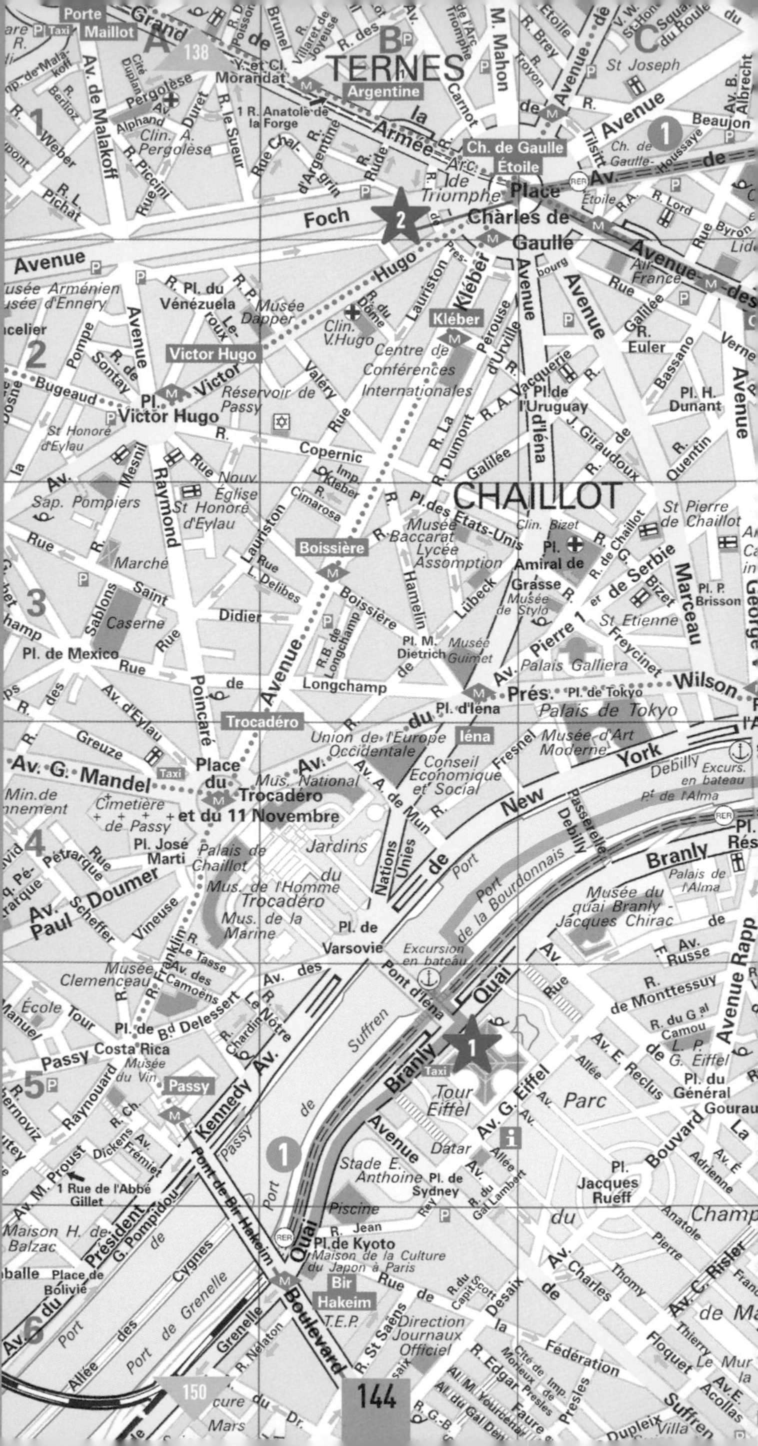
A
B
C
138
150
1
2
3
4
5
6
TERNES
CHAILLOT
Porte Maillot
Argentine
Ch. de Gaulle Étoile
Kléber
Victor Hugo
Boissière
Trocadéro
Iéna
Passy
Bir Hakeim
Place Charles de Gaulle
Arc de Triomphe
Avenue Foch
Avenue de la Grande Armée
Av. de Malakoff
Av. Victor Hugo
Pl. Victor Hugo
Avenue Kléber
Avenue d'Iéna
Avenue Marceau
Avenue de New York
Av. Pierre 1er de Serbie
Av. Prés. Wilson
Pl. de Tokyo
Palais de Tokyo
Musée d'Art Moderne
Palais Galliera
Musée Guimet
Pl. d'Iéna
Rue de Longchamp
Avenue Raymond Poincaré
Av. d'Eylau
Pl. de Mexico
Rue de la Pompe
Rue Saint Didier
Rue Copernic
Rue Lauriston
Rue Boissière
Rue Hamelin
Rue de Lübeck
Centre de Conférences Internationales
Réservoir de Passy
Musée Dapper
Musée Arménien
Musée d'Ennery
Pl. du Vénézuela
St Honoré d'Eylau
Nouv. Église St Honoré d'Eylau
Sap. Pompiers
Marché
Caserne
Pl. des États-Unis
Musée Baccarat
Lycée Assomption
Pl. Amiral de Grasse
Musée de Stylo
St Pierre de Chaillot
St Etienne
Pl. de l'Uruguay
Pl. H. Dunant
Pl. M. Dietrich
Union de l'Europe Occidentale
Conseil Économique et Social
Place du Trocadéro et du 11 Novembre
Av. G. Mandel
Cimetière de Passy
Palais de Chaillot
Mus. National
Mus. de l'Homme
Mus. de la Marine
Jardins du Trocadéro
Pl. de Varsovie
Pl. José Marti
Av. Paul Doumer
Musée Clemenceau
Pl. de Costa Rica
Musée du Vin
Maison H. de Balzac
Pl. de Bolivie
Av. du Président Kennedy
Av. du Président G. Pompidou
Pont d'Iéna
Pont de Bir Hakeim
Port de Passy
Port Debilly
Passerelle Debilly
Port de la Bourdonnais
Quai Branly
Musée du quai Branly - Jacques Chirac
Excursion en bateau
Excurs. en bateau
Pt de l'Alma
Palais de l'Alma
Tour Eiffel
Av. G. Eiffel
Parc du Champ de Mars
Stade E. Anthoine
Pl. de Sydney
Piscine
Pl. de Kyoto
Maison de la Culture du Japon à Paris
Pl. Jacques Rueff
Avenue de Suffren
Avenue Bouvard
Av. de la Bourdonnais
Av. Rapp
Pl. du Général Gouraud
Av. E. Reclus
Av. Charles Floquet
Av. de Suffren
Rue de la Fédération
Boulevard de Grenelle
Allée des Cygnes
Port de Grenelle
Direction Journaux Officiel
T.E.P.
1 Rue de l'Abbé Gillet
1 R. Anatole de la Forge
Clin. A. Pergolèse
Clin. V. Hugo
Clin. Bizet
Datar
Air France
St Joseph

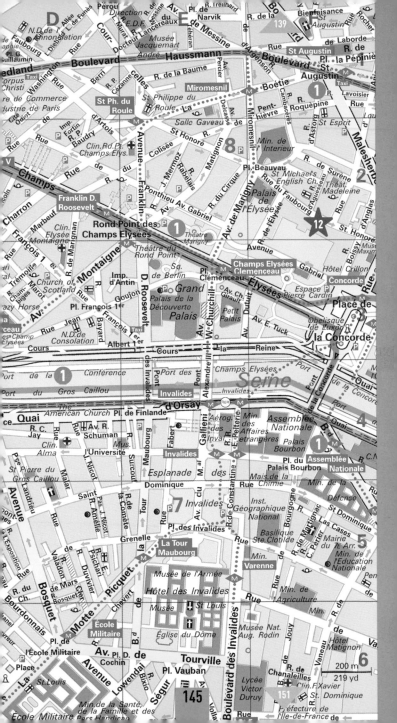

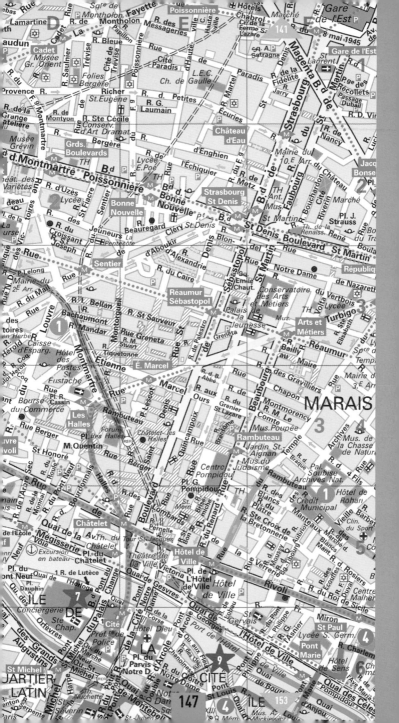

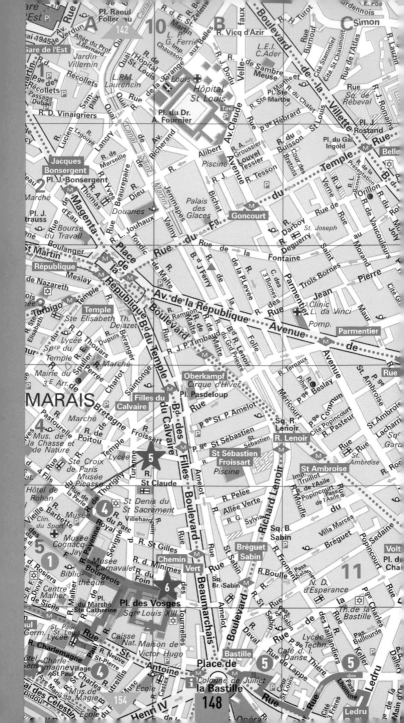

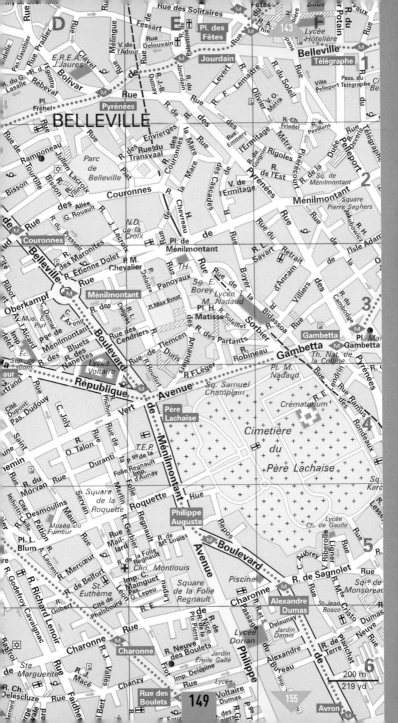

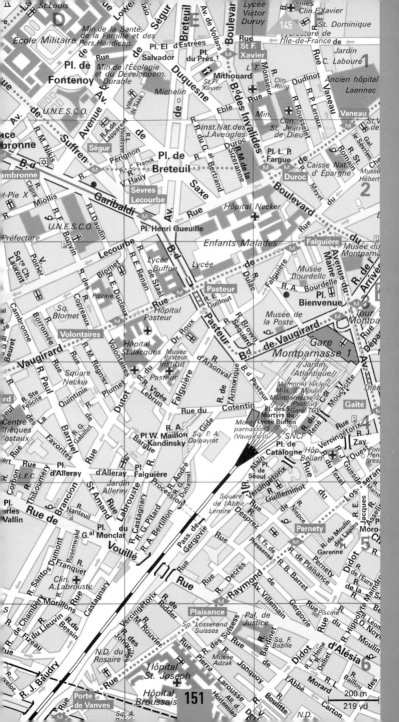

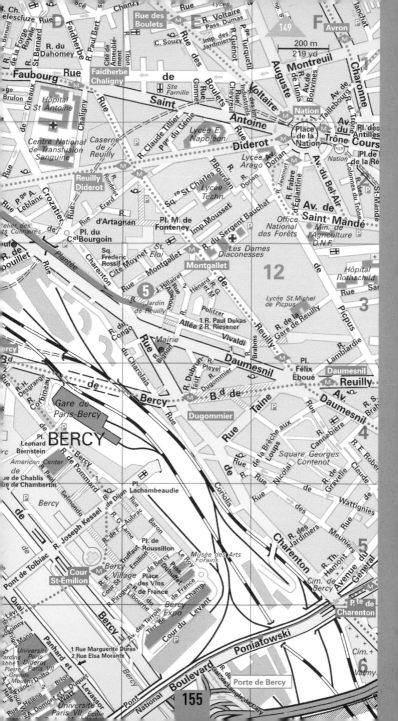

Les Arrondissements de Paris

A · **B** · **C**
1 · **2** · **3** · **4** · **5** · **6**

LA GARENNE-COLOMBES
N 308

COURBEVOIE

ASNIÈRES-S-S

CLICHY

N 310

N 410

Porte de St-Ouen

Seine

Porte de Clichy

N 309

LEVALLOIS-PERRET

Porte d'Asnières

La Défense

Boulevard Circulaire

NEUILLY-S-SEINE

Porte de Champerret

Batignolles 17

PUTEAUX

N 13

Bd. M. Barrès

Palais des Congrès

Gare St-Lazare

Porte Maillot

Porte Dauphine

Arc de Triomphe

Place Charles de Gaulle

Élysée 8

Ste-Marie Madeleine

Bois

N 185

Porte de la Muette

Passy 16

Palais de Chaillot

Palais de l'Élysée

Grand Palais

Petit Palais

Place de la Concorde

Obélisque

Lou

de

Porte de Passy

Maison de Radio France

Tour Eiffel

Palais de Bourbon 7

Quai d'Orsay

Quai des Tuileries

Boulogne

Hippodrome d'Auteuil

Porte d'Auteuil

Hôtel des Invalides

Lu

A 13

Porte Molitor

École Militaire

4

Stade du Parc des Princes

N 307 la Reine

15 Vaugirard

Gare Montparnasse

BOULOGNE-

N 10

Porte de St-Cloud

Observatoire 14

5

BILLANCOURT

N 187

Quai d'Issy

Porte de Sèvres

N 187

ISSY-LES-MOULINEAUX

N 189

Porte de la Plaine

VANVES

Porte Brancion

Porte de Vanves

Porte de Châtillon

MALAKOFF

Porte d'Orléans

N 305

N 20

MONTROUGE

6

MEUDON

CLAMART

CHÂTILLON

Bois de Clamart

156

D

SAINT-OUEN

Av. Michel et
Av. de la Chapelle

Porte de la Chapelle **A1**
N 14

E

AUBERVILLIERS

Porte d'Aubervilliers

Porte de la Villette

F

2 km
1.24 mi

1

Porte de Clignancourt Ney Bd. Macdonald

PANTIN

18
Butte Montmartre
Sacré Cœur

Porte de Pantin
LE PRÉ-ST-GERVAIS
Porte du Pré St-Gervais

R. Méhul
LES LILAS

2

Gare du Nord

19
Buttes Chaumonts

Porte des Lilas

Opéra 9

Opéra National

Gare de l'Est

Enclos-St-Laurent **10**

BAGNOLET
Porte de Bagnolet **3**
A 3

Bourse 2

Place de la République

Ménilmontant
20

MONTREUIL

Palais Royal

Temple **3**
Centre Pompidou

Popincourt
11

St-Ambroise

Palais de Justice

Hôtel de Ville **4**
Notre-Dame

Place de la Bastille

Opéra Bastille

Place de la Nation

Cours de Vincennes N 34

Porte de Montreuil

Porte de Vincennes **4**

Panthéon
5

Gare de Lyon

Reuilly
12

Porte de St-Mandé

ST-MANDÉ

Observatoire

Gare d'Austerlitz

Palais Omnisports de Paris-Bercy

Porte Dorée

Bois
5
de
Vincennes

Gobelins
13

Porte de Charenton

Porte de Bercy

CHARENTON

ST-MAURICE

Marne

6

Porte de Gentilly

A6a **A6b**

GENTILLY LE KRÉMLIN-BICÊTRE

Porte d'Italie N 305

N 7

Porte d'Ivry

IVRY-SUR-SEINE

Pont d'Ivry

A 4

N 6

Seine

ALFORTVILLE

CUEIL

157

STREET INDEX

Autoroute Autobahn		Motorway Autosnelweg
Route à quatre voies Vierspurige Straße		Road with four lanes Weg met vier rijstroken
Route à grande circulation Fernstraße		Trunk road Weg voor interlokaal verkeer
Route principale Hauptstraße		Main road Hoofdweg
Autres routes Sonstige Straßen		Other roads Overige wegen
Rue à sens unique Einbahnstraße		One-way street Straat met eenrichtingsverkeer
Zone piétonne Fußgängerzone		Pedestrian zone Voetgangerszone
Information - Parking Information - Parkplatz	**i** P	Information - Parking place Informatie - Parkeerplaats
Chemin de fer principal avec gare Hauptbahn mit Bahnhof		Main railway with station Belangrijke spoorweg met station
Autre ligne Sonstige Bahn		Other railway Overige spoorweg
Gare RER RER-Bahnhof	RER	RER Station RER Station
Métro U-Bahn	M	Underground Ondergrondse spoorweg
Église remarquable - Autre église Sehenswerte Kirche - Sonstige Kirche		Church of interest - Other church Bezienswaardige kerk - Andere kerk
Synagogue - Mosquée Synagoge - Moschee		Synagogue - Mosque Synagoge - Moskee
Monument - Auberge de jeunesse Denkmal - Jugendherberge		Monument - Youth hostel Monument - Jeugdherberg
Poste de police - Bureau de poste Polizeistation - Postamt		Police station - Post office Politiebureau - Postkantoor
Hôpital - Bus d'aéroport Krankenhaus - Flughafenbus	B	Hospital - Airport bus Ziekenhuis - Vliegveldbus
Zone bâtie, bâtiment public Bebauung, öffentliches Gebäude		Built-up area, public building Woongebied, openbaar gebouw
Zone industrielle Industriegelände		Industrial area Industrieterrein
Parc, bois - Cimetière Park, Wald - Friedhof	+ + + + + +	Park, forest - Cemetery Park, bos - Kerkhof
MARCO POLO Tour d'aventure 1 MARCO POLO Erlebnistour 1		MARCO POLO Discovery Tour 1 MARCO POLO Avontuurlijke Route 1
MARCO POLO Tours d'aventure MARCO POLO Erlebnistouren		MARCO POLO Discovery Tours MARCO POLO Avontuurlijke Routes
MARCO POLO Highlight	★	MARCO POLO Highlight

FOR YOUR NEXT TRIP...

MARCO POLO TRAVEL GUIDES

INDEX

This index lists all the sites and excursion destinations as well as important streets and squares referenced in the travel guide. Page numbers in bold type refer to the main entry listing.

WRITE TO US

e-mail: info@marcopologuides.co.uk

Did you have a great holiday?
Is there something on your mind?
Whatever it is, let us know!
Whether you want to praise, alert us
to errors or give us a personal tip –
MARCO POLO would be pleased to
hear from you.
We do everything we can to provide
the very latest information for your trip.

Nevertheless, despite all of our authors'
thorough research, errors can creep
in. MARCO POLO does not accept any
liability for this. Please contact us by
e-mail or post.

MARCO POLO Travel Publishing Ltd
Pinewood, Chineham Business Park
Crockford Lane, Chineham
Basingstoke, Hampshire RG24 8AL
United Kingdom

PICTURE CREDITS
Cover Photograph: Sacre-Cœur (Look/NordicPhotos)
Photographs: R. Freyer (44, 84); R. M. Gill (30, 78, 118, 118/119, 119, 122 top); huber-images: A. Bartuccio (14/15), S. Bozzi (2), F. Carovillano (9), Cristofori (50), Damm (122 bottom), Gräfenhain (134/135), Kremer (36/37), S. Kremer (flap left, 17, 52, 58/59, 111), H. - P. Merten (102/103), A. Saffo (56); H. Krinitz (10, 47, 48, 55, 62, 120, 121); Laif: P. Adenis (8), T. Dorn (7), Galli (123), P. Wallet (65); Laif/hemis.fr: Escudero (66), B. Gardel (60/61), F. Guiziou (101), H. Hughes (97), M. Renaudeau (98), Sonnet (4 bottom, 72/73); Laif/Le Figaro Magazine: Martin (92/93); Laif/RAPHO (91); Laif/Tripe-lon: Jarry (71); Look/age fotostock (12/13); Look/NordicPhotos (1); mauritius images/age (42, 46); mauritius images/Alamy (flap right, 3, 4 top, 11, 18 top, 18 centre, 19 top, 20/21, 26/27, 54, 70 right, 74, 77, 79, 81, 87, 108, 117), T. French (6), J. Gil (82/83), J. Kellerman (114), Newzulu (120/121); mauritius images/Alamy/Directphoto Collection (89); mauritius images/Hero Images (19 bottom); mauritius images/imagebroker: J. Thomandl (18 bottom); mauritius images/Masterfile RM. R. Ian Lloyd (24); mauritius images/Robert Harding (23); C. Naundorf (5, 32, 39, 40, 69, 70 left, 94)

4th edition – fully revised and updated 2019
Worldwide Distribution: Marco Polo Travel Publishing Ltd, Pinewood, Chineham Business Park, Crockford Lane, Basingstoke, Hampshire RG24 8AL, United Kingdom. Email: sales@marcopolouk.com
© MAIRDUMONT GmbH & Co. KG, Ostfildern
Chief editor: Marion Zorn; Authors: Gerhard Bläske, Waltraud Pfister-Bläske; Co-author: Felicitas Schwarz; Editor: Arnd M Schuppius; Programme supervision: Lucas Forst-Gill, Susanne Heimburger, Tamara Hub, Johanna Jiranek, Nikolai Michaelis, Kristin Wittemann, Tim Wohlbold; Picture editor: Gabriele Forst
Cartography street atlas: © MAIRDUMONT, Ostfildern; Hallwag Kümmerly+Frey AG, CH-Schönbühl/Bern; Cartography pull-out map: © MAIRDUMONT, Ostfildern
Design front cover, p. 1, pull-out map cover: Karl Anders – Büro für Visual Stories, Hamburg; interior: milchhof:atelier, Berlin; Discovery Tours, p. 2/3: Susan Chaaban Dipl.-Des. (FH)
Translated from German by Jennifer Walcoff Neuheiser, Samantha Riffle;
Prepress: writehouse, Cologne; InterMedia, Ratingen
Phrase book in cooperation with Ernst Klett Sprachen GmbH, Stuttgart,
Editorial by Pons Wörterbücher

DOS & DON'TS ✋

A few things you should bear in mind in Paris

DON'T SEAT YOURSELF AT A RESTAURANT

When you go to a restaurant, don't make a beeline for the nearest table. In Paris it is customary to wait for a waiter to show you to your table. However, you may be able to change tables if the one initially chosen is not to your liking.

DON'T STAND ON THE LEFT SIDE OF AN ESCALATOR

If you stand on the left – the fast lane – of an escalator in one of the Métro stations or department stores, expect Parisians to give you a reproachful look.

DON'T MAKE IT TOO EASY FOR PICKPOCKETS

Always keep your valuables in closed bags, and carry rucksacks and handbags against your belly when you're in large crowds. Never leave your valuables in your jacket pocket when you hang your jacket over your chair in a restaurant or café, and always keep an eye on your luggage.

DON'T STAY SEATED ON THE MÉTRO'S FOLDING SEATS

There are folding seats right next to the doors of the train on many Métro lines. You can use them as long as the Métro is relatively empty, but watch out when it starts to fill up. Don't miss the moment when experienced Métro riders stand up to make room for newly boarded passengers. If you don't stand as well, you risk more than just nasty looks from your fellow passengers; you might also take a handbag or rucksack to the face.

DON'T FALL FOR SCAM ARTISTS

Apart from thimbleriggers, the scam artists of Paris also include deaf-mutes who make you sign a petition and then demand money, boys who offer you counterfeit Métro tickets when you're at the end of a queue, or men who ask you for directions when you withdraw money from a cash machine – their accomplices will swipe the bank notes from the machine whilst you're distracted.

DON'T EAT PIZZA

Although there are exceptions, the quality of pizza in Paris leaves a lot to be desired. Pizzas tend to be doughy, greasy and often lacking in proper ingredients. Only a few are baked in wood-fired ovens even though the prices are predictably high.

DON'T DRIVE IN THE CITY CENTRE

Paris is bogged down with traffic like no other major city. Apart from tourists attempting to get accustomed to the driving style in the city where the law of the jungle applies, massive traffic jams are also a bane for Parisians and a reality in their daily life.